No. 19

by James Madison

The Subject continued, with further Examples

The examples of ancient confederacies, cited in my last paper, have not exhausted the source of experimental instruction on this subject. There are existing institutions, founded on a similar principle, which merit particular consideration. The first which presents itself is the Germanic body.

In the early ages of christianity, Germany was occupied by seven distinct nations, who had no common chief. The Franks, one of the number, having conquered the Gauls, established the kingdom which has taken its name from them. In the ninth century, Charlemagne, its warlike monarch, carried his victorious arms in every direction; and Germany became a part of his vast dominions. On the dismemberment, which took place under his sons, this part was erected into a separate and independent empire. Charlemagne and his immediate descendants possessed the reality, as well as the ensigns and dignity of imperial power. But the principal vassals, whose fiefs had become hereditary, and who composed the national diets, which Charlemagne had not abolished, gradually threw off the yoke, and advanced to sovereign jurisdiction and independence. The force of imperial sovereignty was insufficient to restrain such powerful dependants; or to preserve the unity and tranquillity of the empire. The most furious private wars, accompanied with every species of calamity, were carried on between the different princes and states. The imperial authority, unable to maintain the public order, declined by degrees, till it was almost extinct in the anarchy, which agitated the long interval between the death of the last emperor of the Suabian, and the accession of the first emperor of the Austrian lines. In the eleventh century, the emperors enjoyed full sovereignty: in the fifteenth, they had little more than the symbols and decorations of power.

Out of this feudal system, which has itself many of the important features

HOW TO READ
The Federalist Papers & The Constitution of the United States

(Part 2)

John Jay

James Madison

Alexander Hamilton

presented by
LENA SHIMOMURA

THE FEDERALIST

BY

Alexander Hamilton,

John Jay,

AND

James Madison

No. 19

of a confederacy, has grown the federal system, which constitutes the Germanic empire. Its powers are vested in a diet representing the component members of the confederacy; in the emperor who is the executive magistrate, with a negative on the decrees of the diet; and in the imperial chamber and aulic council, two judiciary tribunals having supreme jurisdiction in controversies which concern the empire, or which happen among its members.

The diet possesses the general power of legislating for the empire; of making war and peace; contracting alliances; assessing quotas of troops and money; constructing fortresses; regulating coin; admitting new members; and subjecting disobedient members to the ban of the empire, by which the party is degraded from his sovereign rights, and his possessions forfeited. The members of the confederacy are expressly restricted from entering into compacts, prejudicial to the empire; from imposing tolls and duties on their mutual intercourse, without the consent of the emperor and diet; from altering the value of money; from doing injustice to one another; or from affording assistance or retreat to disturbers of the public peace. And the ban is denounced against such as shall violate any of these restrictions. The members of the diet, as such, are subject in all cases to be judged by the emperor and diet, and in their private capacities by the aulic council and imperial chamber.

The prerogatives of the emperor are numerous. The most important of them are, his exclusive right to make propositions to the diet; to negative its resolutions; to name ambassadors; to confer dignities and titles; to fill vacant electorates; to found universities; to grant privileges not injurious to the states of the empire; to receive and apply the public revenues; and generally to watch over the public safety. In certain cases, the electors form a council to him. In quality of emperor, he possesses no territory within the empire; nor receives any revenue for his support. But his revenue and dominions, in other qualities, constitute him one of the most powerful princes in Europe.

From such a parade of constitutional powers, in the representatives and head of this confederacy, the natural supposition would be, that it must form an exception to the general character which belongs to its kindred systems. Nothing would be further from the reality. The fundamental principle, on which it rests, that the empire is a community of sovereigns; that the diet is a representation of sovereigns; and that the laws are addressed to sovereigns; render the empire a nerveless body, incapable of regulating its own members, insecure against external dangers, and agitated with unceasing fermentations in its own bowels.

The history of Germany, is a history of wars between the emperor and the princes and states; of wars among the princes and states themselves; of the licentiousness of the strong, and the oppression of the weak; of foreign intrusions, and foreign intrigues; of requisitions of men and money disregarded, or partially complied with; of attempts to enforce them, altogether abortive, or attended with slaughter and desolation, involving the innocent with the guilty; of general imbecility, confusion, and misery.

In the sixteenth century, the emperor, with one part of the empire on his side, was seen engaged against the other princes and states. In one of the conflicts, the emperor himself was put to flight, and very near being made prisoner by the elector of Saxony. The late king of Prussia was more than once pitted against his imperial sovereign; and commonly proved an overmatch for him. Controversies and wars among the members themselves, have been so common, that the German annals are crowded with the bloody pages which describe them. Previous to the peace of Westphalia, Germany was desolated by a war of thirty years, in which the emperor, with one half of the empire, was on one side; and Sweden, with the other half, on the opposite side. Peace was at length negotiated, and dictated by foreign powers; and the articles of it, to which foreign powers are parties, made a fundamental part of the Germanic constitution.

If the nation happens, on any emergency, to be more united by the necessity of self-defence, its situation is still deplorable. Military preparations must be preceded by so many tedious discussions, arising from the jealousies, pride, separate views, and clashing pretensions, of sovereign bodies, that before the diet can settle the arrangements, the enemy are in the field; and before the federal troops are ready to take it, are retiring into winter quarters.

The small body of national troops, which has been judged necessary in time of peace, is defectively kept up, badly paid, infected with local prejudices, and supported by irregular and disproportionate contributions to the treasury.

The impossibility of maintaining order, and dispensing justice among these sovereign subjects, produced the experiment of dividing the empire into nine or ten circles or districts; of giving them an interior organization, and of charging them with the military execution of the laws against delinquent and contumacious members. This experiment has only served to demonstrate more fully, the radical vice of the constitution. Each circle is the miniature picture of the deformities of this political monster. They either fail to execute their commissions, or they do it with all the devastation and carnage of civil war. Sometimes whole circles are defaulters; and then they increase the mischief which they were instituted to remedy.

We may form some judgment of this scheme of military coercion, from a sample given by Thuanus. In Donawerth, a free and imperial city of the circle of Suabia, the abbe de St. Croix enjoyed certain immunities which had been reserved to him. In the exercise of these, on some public occasion, outrages were committed on him, by the people of the city. The consequence was, that the city was put under the ban of the empire; and the duke of Bavaria, though director of another circle, obtained an appointment to enforce it. He soon appeared before the city, with a corps of ten thousand troops; and finding it a fit occasion, as he had secretly intended from the beginning, to revive an antiquated claim, on the pretext that his ancestors had suffered the place to be dismembered from his territory;* he took possession of it in his own name; disarmed and punished the inhabitants, and re-annexed the city to his domains.

It may be asked, perhaps, what has so long kept this disjointed machine from falling entirely to pieces? The answer is obvious. The weakness of most of the members, who are unwilling to expose themselves to the mercy of foreign powers; the weakness of most of the principal members, compared with the formidable powers all around them; the vast weight and influence which the emperor derives from his separate and hereditary dominions; and the interest he feels in preserving a system with which his family pride is connected, and which constitutes him the first prince in Europe: these causes support a feeble and precarious union; whilst the repellent quality, incident to the nature of sovereignty, and which time continually strengthens, prevents any reform whatever, founded on a proper consolidation. Nor is it to be imagined, if this obstacle could be surmounted, that the neighbouring powers would suffer a revolution to take place, which would give to the empire the force and pre-eminence to which it is entitled. Foreign nations have long considered

---

*Pfeffel, Nouvel abreg. chronol. de l'hist. etc. d'Allemagne, says, the pretext was to indemnify himself for the expense of the expedition.

themselves as interested in the changes made by events in this constitution; and have, on various occasions, betrayed their policy of perpetuating its anarchy and weakness.

If more direct examples were wanting, Poland, as a government over local sovereigns, might not improperly be taken notice of. Nor could any proof, more striking, be given of the calamities flowing from such institutions. Equally unfit for self-government, and self-defence, it has long been at the mercy of its powerful neighbours; who have lately had the mercy to disburden it of one third of its people and territories.

The connexion among the Swiss cantons, scarcely amounts to a confederacy; though it is sometimes cited as an instance of the stability of such institutions.

They have no common treasury; no common troops even in war; no common coin; no common judicatory, nor any other common mark of sovereignty.

They are kept together by the peculiarity of their topographical position; by their individual weakness and insignificancy; by the fear of powerful neighbours, to one of which they were formerly subject; by the few sources of contention among a people of such simple and homogeneous manners; by their joint interest in their dependent possessions; by the mutual aid they stand in need of, for suppressing insurrections and rebellions; an aid expressly stipulated, and often required and afforded; and by the necessity of some regular and permanent provision for accommodating disputes among the cantons. The provision is, that the parties at variance shall each choose four judges out of the neutral cantons, who, in case of disagreement, choose an umpire. This tribunal, under an oath of impartiality, pronounces definitive sentence, which all the cantons are bound to enforce. The competency of this regulation may be estimated by a clause in their treaty of 1683, with Victor Amadeus of Savoy; in which he obliges himself to interpose as mediator in disputes between the cantons; and to employ force, if necessary, against the contumacious party.

So far as the peculiarity of their case will admit of comparison with that of the United States, it serves to confirm the principle intended to be established. Whatever efficacy the union may have had in ordinary cases, it appears that the moment a cause of difference sprang up, capable of trying its strength, it failed. The controversies on the subject of religion, which in three instances have kindled violent and bloody contests, may be said in fact to have severed the league. The Protestant and Catholic cantons, have since had their separate diets; where all the most important concerns are adjusted, and which have left the general diet little other business than to take care of the common bailages.

That separation had another consequence, which merits attention. It produced opposite alliances with foreign powers: of Bern, as the head of the Protestant association, with the United Provinces; and of Luzerne, as the head of the Catholic association, with France.

PUBLIUS

No. 20

by James Madison

The Subject continued, with further Examples

The United Netherlands are a confederacy of republics, or rather of aristocracies, of a very remarkable texture; yet confirming all the lessons derived from those which we have already reviewed.

The union is composed of seven co-equal and sovereign states, and each state or province is a composition of equal and independent cities. In all important cases, not only the provinces, but the cities, must be unanimous.

The sovereignty of the union is represented by the states-general, consisting usually of about fifty deputies appointed by the provinces. They hold their seats, some for life, some for six, three, and one years. From two provinces they continue in appointment during pleasure.

The states-general have authority to enter into treaties and alliances; to make war and peace; to raise armies and equip fleets; to ascertain quotas and demand contributions. In all these cases, however, unanimity and the sanction of their constituents are requisite. They have authority to appoint and receive ambassadors; to execute treaties and alliances already formed; to provide for the collection of duties on imports and exports; to regulate the mint, with a saving to the provincial rights; to govern as sovereigns the dependent territories. The provinces are restrained, unless with the general consent, from entering into foreign treaties; from establishing imposts injurious to others, or charging their neighbours with higher duties than their own subjects. A council of state, a chamber of accounts, with five colleges of admiralty, aid and fortify the federal administration.

The executive magistrate of the union is the stadtholder, who is now an hereditary prince. His principal weight and influence in the republic are derived from his independent title; from his great patrimonial estates; from his family connexions with some of the chief potentates of Europe; and more than all, perhaps, from his being stadtholder in the several provinces, as well as for the union; in which provincial quality, he has the appointment of town magistrates under certain regulations, executes provincial decrees, presides when he pleases in the provincial tribunals; and has throughout the power of pardon.

As stadtholder of the union, he has, however, considerable prerogatives.

In his political capacity, he has authority to settle disputes between the provinces, when other methods fail; to assist at the deliberations of the states-general, and at their particular conferences; to give audiences to foreign ambassadors, and to keep agents for his particular affairs at foreign courts.

In his military capacity, he commands the federal troops; provides for garrisons, and in general regulates military affairs; disposes of all appointments from colonels to ensigns, and of the governments and posts of fortified towns.

In his marine capacity, he is admiral general, and superintends and directs every thing relative to naval forces, and other naval affairs; presides in the admiralties in person or by proxy; appoints lieutenant admirals and other officers; and establishes councils of war, whose sentences are not executed till he approves them.

His revenue, exclusive of his private income, amounts to 300,000 florins. The standing army which he commands consists of about 40,000 men.

Such is the nature of the celebrated Belgic confederacy, as delineated on parchment. What are the characters which practice has stampt upon it? Imbecility in the government; discord among the provinces; foreign influence and indignities; a precarious existence in peace, and peculiar calamities from war.

It was long ago remarked by Grotius, that nothing but the hatred of his countrymen to the house of Austria, kept them from being ruined by the vices of their constitution.

The union of Utrecht, says another respectable writer, reposes an authority in the states-general, seemingly sufficient to secure harmony; but the jealousy in each province renders the practice very different from the theory.

The same instrument, says another, obliges each province to levy certain contributions; but this article never could, and probably never will, be executed; because the inland provinces, who have little commerce, cannot pay an equal quota.

In matters of contribution, it is the practice to wa[i]ve the articles of the constitution. The danger of delay obliges the consenting provinces to furnish their quotas, without waiting for the others; and then to obtain reimbursement from the others, by deputations, which are frequent, or otherwise, as they can. The great wealth and influence of the province of Holland, enable her to effect both these purposes.

It has more than once happened that the deficiencies have been ultimately to be collected at the point of the bayonet; a thing practicable, though dreadful, in a confederacy, where one of the members exceeds in force all the rest; and where several of them are too small to meditate resistance: but utterly impracticable in one composed of members, several of which are equal to each other in strength and resources, and equal singly to a vigorous and persevering defence.

Foreign ministers, says Sir William Temple, who was himself a foreign minister, elude matters taken *ad referendum,* by tampering with the provinces and cities. In 1726, the treaty of Hanover was delayed by these means a whole year. Instances of a like nature are numerous and notorious.

In critical emergencies, the states-general are often compelled to overleap their constitutional bounds. In 1688, they concluded a treaty of themselves, at the risk of their heads. The treaty of Westphalia in 1648, by which their independence was formally and finally recognized, was concluded without the consent of Zealand. Even as recently as the last treaty of peace with Great Britain, the constitutional principle of unanimity was departed from. A weak constitution must necessarily terminate in dissolution, for want of proper powers, or the usurpation of powers requisite for the public safety. Whether the usurpation, when once begun, will stop at the salutary point, or go forward to the dangerous extreme, must depend on the contingencies of the moment. Tyranny has perhaps oftener grown out of the assumptions of power, called for, on pressing exigencies, by a defective constitution, than out of the full exercise of the largest constitutional authorities.

Notwithstanding the calamities produced by the stadtholdership, it has been supposed, that without his influence in the individual provinces, the causes of anarchy manifest in the confederacy, would long ago have dissolved it. "Under such a government," says the abbe Mably, "the union could never have subsisted, if the provinces had not a spring within themselves, capable of quickening their tardiness, and compelling them to the same way of thinking. This spring is the stadtholder." It is remarked by Sir William Temple, that "in the intermissions of the stadtholdership, Holland, by her riches and her authority, which drew the others into a sort of dependence, supplied the place."

These are not the only circumstances which have controled the tendency to anarchy and dissolution. The surrounding powers impose an absolute necessity of union to a certain degree, at the same time that they nourish, by their intrigues, the constitutional vices, which keep the republic in some degree always at their mercy.

The true patriots have long bewailed the fatal tendency of these vices, and have made no less than four regular experiments by *extraordinary assemblies,* convened for the special purpose, to apply a remedy. As many times, has their laudable zeal found it impossible to *unite the public councils* in reforming the known, the acknowledged, the fatal evils of the existing constitution. Let us pause, my fellow citizens, for one moment, over this melancholy and monitory lesson of history; and with the tear that drops for the calamities brought on mankind by their adverse opinions and selfish passions, let our gratitude mingle an ejaculation to Heaven, for the propitious concord which has distinguished the consultations for our political happiness.

A design was also conceived, of establishing a general tax to be administered by the federal authority. This also had its adversaries and failed.

This unhappy people seem to be now suffering, from popular convulsions, from dissentions among the states, and from the actual invasion of foreign arms, the crisis of their destiny. All nations have their eyes fixed on the awful spectacle. The first wish prompted by humanity is, that this severe trial may issue in such a revolution of their government, as will establish their union, and render it the parent of tranquillity, freedom, and happiness: the next, that the asylum under which, we trust, the enjoyment of these blessings will speedily be secured in this country, may receive and console them for the catastrophe of their own.

I make no apology for having dwelt so long on the contemplation of these federal precedents. Experience is the oracle of truth; and where its responses are unequivocal, they ought to be conclusive and sacred. The important truth, which it unequivocally pronounces in the present case, is, that a sovereignty over sovereigns, a government over governments, a legislation for communities, as contradistinguished from individuals; as it is a solecism in theory, so in practice, it is subversive of the order and ends of civil polity, by substituting *violence* in place of *law*, or the destructive *coercion* of the *sword*, in place of the mild and salutary *coercion* of the *magistracy*.

PUBLIUS

No. 21

by Alexander Hamilton

Further defects of the present Constitution

Having in the three last numbers taken a summary review of the principal circumstances and events, which depict the genius and fate of other confederate governments; I shall now proceed in the enumeration of the most important of those defects, which have hitherto disappointed our hopes from the system established among ourselves. To form a safe and satisfactory judgment of the proper remedy, it is absolutely necessary that we should be well acquainted with the extent and malignity of the disease.

The next most palpable defect of the existing confederation, is the total want of a SANCTION to its laws. The United States, as now composed, have no power to exact obedience, or punish disobedience to their resolutions, either by pecuniary mulcts, by a suspension or divestiture of privileges, or by any other constitutional means. There is no express delegation of authority to them to use force against delinquent members; and if such a right should be ascribed to the federal head, as resulting from the nature of the social compact between the states, it must be by inference and construction, in the face of that part of the second article, by which it is declared, "that each state shall retain every power, jurisdiction, and right, not *expressly* delegated to the United States in Congress assembled." The want of such a right involves, no doubt, a striking absurdity; but we are reduced to the dilemma, either of supposing that deficiency, preposterous as it may seem, or of contravening or explaining away a provision, which has been of late a repeated theme of the eulogies of those who oppose the new constitution; and the omission of which, in that plan, has been the subject of much plausible animadversion, and severe criticism. If we are unwilling to impair the force of this applauded provision, we shall be obliged to conclude, that the United States afford the extraordinary spectacle of a government, destitute even of the shadow of constitutional power, to enforce the execution of its own laws. It will appear, from the specimens which have been cited, that the American confederacy, in this particular, stands discriminated from every other institution of a similar kind, and exhibits a new and unexampled phenomenon in the political world.

The want of a mutual guarantee of the state governments, is another capital imperfection in the federal plan. There is nothing of this kind declared in the articles that compose it: and to imply a tacit guarantee from considerations of utility, would be a still more flagrant departure from the clause which has been mentioned, than to imply a tacit power of coercion, from the like consideration. The want of a guarantee, though it might in its consequences endanger the union, does not so immediately attack its existence, as the want of a constitutional sanction to its laws.

Without a guarantee, the assistance to be derived from the union, in repelling those domestic dangers, which may sometimes threaten the existence of the state constitutions, must be renounced. Usurpation may rear its crest in each state, and trample upon the liberties of the people; while the national government could legally do nothing more than behold its encroachments with indignation and regret. A successful faction may erect a tyranny on the ruins of order and law, while no succour could constitutionally be afforded by the union to the friends and supporters of the government. The tempestuous situation from which Massachusetts has scarcely emerged, evinces, that dangers of this kind are not merely speculative. Who can determine what might have been the issue of her late convulsions, if the malcontents had been headed by a Caesar or by a Cromwell? Who can predict what effect a despotism, established in Massachusetts, would have upon the liberties of New Hampshire or Rhode Island; of Connecticut or New York?

The inordinate pride of state importance, has suggested to some minds an objection to the principle of a guarantee in the federal government, as involving an officious interference in the domestic concerns of the members. A scruple of this kind would deprive us of one of the principal advantages to be expected from union; and can only flow from a misapprehension of the nature of the provision itself. It could be no impediment to reforms of the state constitutions by a majority of the people in a legal and peaceable mode. This right would remain undiminished. The guarantee could only operate against changes to be effected by violence. Towards the prevention of calamities of this kind, too many checks cannot be provided. The peace of society, and the stability of government, depend absolutely on the efficacy of the precautions adopted on this head. Where the whole power of the government is in the hands of the people, there is the less pretence for the use of violent remedies, in partial or occasional distempers of the state. The natural cure for an ill administration, in a popular or representative constitution, is, a change of men. A guarantee by the national authority, would be as much directed against the usurpations of rulers, as against the ferments and outrages of faction and sedition in the community.

The principle of regulating the contributions of the states to the common treasury by QUOTAS, is another fundamental error in the confederation. Its repugnancy to an adequate supply of the national exigencies, has been already pointed out, and has sufficiently appeared from the trial which has been made of it. I speak of it now solely with a view to equality among the states. Those who have been accustomed to contemplate the circumstances, which produce and constitute national wealth, must be satisfied that there is no common standard, or barometer, by which the degrees of it can be ascertained. Neither the value of lands, nor the numbers of the people, which have been successively proposed as the rule of state contributions, has any pretension to being a just representative. If we compare the wealth of the United Netherlands with that of Russia or Germany, or even of France; and if we at the same time compare the total value of the lands, and the aggregate population of the contracted territory of that republic, with the total value of the lands, and the aggregate population of the immense regions of either of those kingdoms, we shall at once discover, that there is no comparison between the proportion of either of these two objects, and that of the relative wealth of those nations. If the like parallel were to be run between several of the American states, it would furnish a like result. Let Virginia be contrasted with North Carolina, Pennsylvania with Connecticut, or Maryland with New Jersey, and we shall be convinced that the respective abilities of those states, in relation to revenue, bear little or no analogy to their comparative stock in lands, or to their comparative population. The position may be equally illustrated, by a similar process between the counties of the same state. No man acquainted with the state of New York will doubt, that the active wealth of King's county bears a much greater proportion to that of Montgomery, than it would appear to do, if we should take either the total value of the lands, or the total numbers of the people, as a criterion.

The wealth of nations depends upon an infinite variety of causes. Situation, soil, climate, the nature of the productions, the nature of the government, the genius of the citizens; the degree of information they possess; the state of commerce, of arts, of industry; these circumstances, and many more too complex, minute, or adventitious, to admit of a particular specification, occasion differences hardly conceivable in the relative opulence and riches of different countries. The consequence clearly is, that there can be no common measure of national wealth; and of course, no general or stationary rule, by which the ability of a state to pay taxes can be determined. The attempt, therefore, to regulate the contributions of the members of a confederacy, by any such rule, cannot fail to be productive of glaring inequality, and extreme oppression.

This inequality would of itself be sufficient in America to work the eventual destruction of the union, if any mode of enforcing a compliance with its requisitions could be devised. The suffering states would not long consent to remain associated upon a principle which distributed the public burthens with so unequal a hand; and which was calculated to impoverish and oppress the citizens of some states, while those of others would scarcely be conscious of the small proportion of the weight they were required to sustain. This, however, is an evil inseparable from the principle of quotas and requisitions.

There is no method of steering clear of this inconvenience, but by authorizing the national government to raise its own revenues in its own way. Imposts, excises, and in general all duties upon articles of consumption, may be compared to a fluid, which will in time find its level with the means of paying them. The amount to be contributed by each citizen will in a degree be at his own option, and can be regulated by an attention to his resources. The rich may be extravagant . . . the poor can be frugal: and private oppression may always be avoided, by a judicious selection of objects proper for such impositions. If inequalities should arise in some states from duties on particular objects, these will, in all probability, be counterbalanced by proportional inequalities in other states, from the duties on other objects. In the course of time and things, an equilibrium, as far as it is attainable, in so complicated a subject, will be established every where. Or if inequalities should still exist, they would neither be so great in their degree, so uniform in their operation, nor so odious in their appearance, as those which would necessarily spring from quotas, upon any scale that can possibly be devised.

It is a signal advantage of taxes on articles of consumption, that they contain in their own nature a security against excess. They prescribe their own limit; which cannot be exceeded without defeating the end proposed . . . that is, an extension of the revenue. When applied to this object, the saying is as just as it is witty, that "in political arithmetic, two and two do not always make four." If duties are too high, they lessen the consumption; the collection is eluded; and the product to the treasury is not so great as when they are confined within proper and moderate bounds.

This forms a complete barrier against any material oppression of the citizens, by taxes of this class, and is itself a natural limitation of the power of imposing them.

Impositions of this kind usually fall under the denomination of indirect taxes, and must for a long time constitute the chief part of the revenue raised in this country. Those of the direct kind, which principally relate to lands and buildings, may admit of a rule of apportionment. Either the value of land, or the number of the people, may serve as a standard. The state of agriculture, and the populousness of a country, are considered as having a near relation to each other. And as a rule for the purpose intended, numbers in the view of simplicity and certainty are entitled to a preference. In every country it is an Herculean task to obtain a valuation of the land: in a country imperfectly settled and progressive in improvement, the difficulties are increased almost to impracticability. The expense of an accurate valuation, is in all situations a formidable objection. In a branch of taxation where no limits to the discretion of the government are to be found in the nature of the thing, the establishment of a fixed rule, not incompatible with the end, may be attended with fewer inconveniences than to leave that discretion altogether at large.

PUBLIUS

No. 22

by Alexander Hamilton

The same subject continued, and concluded

In addition to the defects of the existing federal system, enumerated in the last number, there are others of not less importance, which concur in rendering that system altogether unfit for the administration of the affairs of the union.

The want of a power to regulate commerce, is by all parties allowed to be of the number. The utility of such a power has been anticipated under the first head of our inquiries; and for this reason, as well as from the universal conviction entertained upon the subject, little need be added in this place. It is indeed evident, on the most superficial view, that there is no object, either as it respects the interests of trade or finance, that more strongly demands a federal superintendence. The want of it has already operated as a bar to the formation of beneficial treaties with foreign powers; and has given occasions of dissatisfaction between the states. No nation acquainted with the nature of our political association, would be unwise enough to enter into stipulations with the United States, conceding on their part privileges of importance, while they were apprized that the engagements on the part of the union, might at any moment be violated by its members; and while they found, from experience, that they might enjoy every advantage they desired in our markets, without granting us any return, but such as their momentary convenience might suggest. It is not, therefore, to be wondered at, that Mr. Jenkinson, in ushering into the house of commons a bill for regulating the temporary intercourse between the two countries, should preface its introduction by a declaration, that similar provisions in former bills had been found to answer every purpose to the commerce of Great Britain, and that it would be prudent to persist in the plan until it should appear whether the American government was likely or not to acquire greater consistency.*

Several states have endeavoured, by separate prohibitions, restrictions, and exclusions, to influence the conduct of that kingdom in this particular; but the want of concert, arising from the want of a general authority, and from clashing and dissimilar views in the states, has hitherto frustrated every experiment of the kind; and will continue to do so, as long as the same obstacles to an uniformity of measures continue to exist.

The interfering and unneighbourly regulations of some states, contrary to the true spirit of the union, have, in different instances, given just cause of umbrage and complaint to others; and it is to be feared that examples of this nature, if not restrained by a national control, would be multiplied and extended till they became not less serious sources of animosity and discord, than injurious impediments to the intercourse between the different parts of the confederacy. "The commerce of the German empire† is in continual trammels, from the multiplicity of the duties which the several princes and states exact upon the merchandises passing through their territories; by means of which the fine streams and navigable rivers with which Germany is so happily watered, are rendered almost useless." Though the genius of the people of this country might never permit this description to be strictly applicable to us, yet we may reasonably expect, from the gradual conflicts of state regulations, that the citizens of each would at length come to be considered and treated by the others in no better light than that of foreigners and aliens.

The power of raising armies, by the most obvious construction of the articles of the confederation, is merely a power of making requisitions upon the states for quotas of men. This practice, in the course of the late war, was found replete with obstructions to a vigorous, and to an economical system of defence. It gave birth to a competition between the states, which created a kind of auction for men. In order to furnish the quotas required of them, they

---

*This, as nearly as I can recollect, was the sense of this speech on introducing the last bill.
†Encyclopedia, article Empire.

outbid each other, till bounties grew to an enormous and insupportable size. The hope of a still further increase, afforded an inducement to those who were disposed to serve, to procrastinate their enlistment; and disinclined them from engaging for any considerable periods. Hence, slow and scanty levies of men, in the most critical emergencies of our affairs; short enlistments at an unparalleled expense; continual fluctuations in the troops, ruinous to their discipline, and subjecting the public safety frequently to the perilous crisis of a disbanded army. Hence also, those oppressive expedients for raising men, which were upon several occasions practised, and which nothing but the enthusiasm of liberty would have induced the people to endure.

This method of raising troops is not more unfriendly to economy and vigour, than it is to an equal distribution of the burthen. The states near the seat of war, influenced by motives of self-preservation, made efforts to furnish their quotas, which even exceeded their abilities; while those at a distance from danger were, for the most part, as remiss as the others were diligent, in their exertions. The immediate pressure of this inequality was not, in this case, as in that of the contributions of money, alleviated by the hope of a final liquidation. The states which did not pay their proportions of money, might at least be charged with their deficiencies; but no account could be formed of the deficiencies in the supplies of men. We shall not, however, see much reason to regret the want of this hope, when we consider how little prospect there is, that the most delinquent states ever will be able to make compensation for their pecuniary failures. The system of quotas and requisitions, whether it be applied to men or money, is, in every view, a system of imbecility in the union, and of inequality and injustice among the members.

The right of equal suffrage among the states, is another exceptionable part of the confederation. Every idea of proportion, and every rule of fair representation, conspire to condemn a principle, which gives to Rhode Island an equal weight in the scale of power with Massachusetts, or Connecticut, or New York; and to Delaware, an equal voice in the national deliberations with Pennsylvania, or Virginia, or North Carolina. Its operation contradicts that fundamental maxim of republican government, which requires that the sense of the majority should prevail. Sophistry may reply, that sovereigns are equal, and that a majority of the votes of the states will be a majority of confederated America. But this kind of logical legerdemain will never counteract the plain suggestions of justice and common sense. It may happen, that this majority of states is a small minority of the people of America;* and two thirds of the people of America could not long be persuaded, upon the credit of artificial distinctions and syllogistic subtleties, to submit their interests to the management and disposal of one third. The larger states would, after a while, revolt from the idea of receiving the law from the smaller. To acquiesce in such a privation of their due importance in the political scale, would be, not merely to be insensible to the love of power, but even to sacrifice the desire of equality. It is neither rational to expect the first, nor just to require the last. Considering how peculiarly the safety and welfare of the smaller states depend on union, they ought readily to renounce a pretension, which, if not relinquished, would prove fatal to its duration.

It may be objected to this, that not seven, but nine states, or two thirds of the whole number, must consent to the most important resolutions; and it may be thence inferred, that nine states would always comprehend a majority of the inhabitants of the union. But this does not obviate the impropriety of an equal vote, between states of the most unequal dimensions and populousness: nor is the inference accurate in point of fact; for we can enumerate nine states, which contain less than a majority of the people;† and it is constitutionally possible, that these nine may give the vote. Besides, there are matters of considerable moment determinable by a bare majority; and there are others, concerning which doubts have been entertained, which, if interpreted in favour of the sufficiency of a vote of seven states, would extend its operation to interests of the first magnitude. In addition to this, it is to be observed, that there is a probability of an increase in the number of states, and no provision for a proportional augmentation of the ratio of votes.

But this is not all: what, at first sight, may seem a remedy, is, in reality, a poison. To give a minority a negative upon the majority, which is always the case where more than a majority is requisite to a decision, is, in its tendency, to subject the sense of the greater number to that of the lesser. Congress, from the non-attendance of a few states, have been frequently in the situation of a

---

*New Hampshire, Rhode Island, New Jersey, Delaware, Georgia, South Carolina, and Maryland, are a majority of the whole number of the States, but they do not contain one third of the people.

†Add New York and Connecticut to the foregoing seven, and they will still be less than a majority.

Polish diet, where a single VETO has been sufficient to put a stop to all their movements. A sixtieth part of the union, which is about the proportion of Delaware and Rhode Island, has several times been able to oppose an entire bar to its operations. This is one of those refinements, which, in practice, has an effect the reverse of what is expected from it in theory. The necessity of unanimity in public bodies, or of something approaching towards it, has been founded upon a supposition that it would contribute to security. But its real operation is, to embarrass the administration, to destroy the energy of government, and to substitute the pleasure, caprice, or artifices of an insignificant, turbulent, or corrupt junto, to the regular deliberations and decisions of a respectable majority. In those emergencies of a nation, in which the goodness or badness, the weakness or strength of its government, is of the greatest importance, there is commonly a necessity for action. The public business must, in some way or other, go forward. If a pertinacious minority can control the opinion of a majority, respecting the best mode of conducting it, the majority, in order that something may be done, must conform to the views of the minority; and thus the sense of the smaller number will overrule that of the greater, and give a tone to the national proceedings. Hence, tedious delays; continual negotiation and intrigue; contemptible compromises of the public good. And yet, in such a system, it is even fortunate when such compromises can take place: for, upon some occasions, things will not admit of accommodation; and then the measures of government must be injuriously suspended, or fatally defeated. It is often, by the impracticability of obtaining the concurrence of the necessary number of votes, kept in a state of inaction. Its situation must always savour of weakness; sometimes border upon anarchy.

It is not difficult to discover, that a principle of this kind gives greater scope to foreign corruption, as well as to domestic faction, than that which permits the sense of the majority to decide; though the contrary of this has been presumed. The mistake has proceeded from not attending with due care to the mischiefs that may be occasioned, by obstructing the progress of government at certain critical seasons. When the concurrence of a large number is required by the constitution to the doing of any national act, we are apt to rest satisfied that all is safe, because nothing improper will be likely *to be done;* but we forget how much good may be prevented, and how much ill may be produced, by the power of hindering that which it is necessary to do, and of keeping affairs in the same unfavourable posture in which they may happen to stand at particular periods.

Suppose, for instance, we were engaged in a war, in conjunction with one foreign nation, against another. Suppose the necessity of our situation demanded peace, and that the interest or ambition of our ally led him to seek the prosecution of the war, with views that might justify us in making separate terms. In such a state of things, this ally of ours would evidently find it much easier, by his bribes and his intrigues, to tie up the hands of government from making peace, where two thirds of all the votes were requisite to that object, than where a simple majority would suffice. In the first case, he would have to corrupt a smaller . . . in the last, a greater number. Upon the same principle, it would be much easier for a foreign power with which we were at war, to perplex our councils and embarrass our exertions. And in a commercial view, we may be subjected to similar inconveniences. A nation with which we might have a treaty of commerce, could with much greater facility prevent our forming a connexion with her competitor in trade; though such a connexion should be ever so beneficial to ourselves.

Evils of this description ought not to be regarded as imaginary. One of the weak sides of republics, among their numerous advantages, is, that they afford too easy an inlet to foreign corruption. An hereditary monarch, though often disposed to sacrifice his subjects to his ambition, has so great a personal interest in the government, and in the external glory of the nation, that it is not easy for a foreign power to give him an equivalent for what he would sacrifice by treachery to the state. The world has accordingly been witness to few examples of this species of royal prostitution, though there have been abundant specimens of every other kind.

In republics, persons elevated from the mass of the community, by the suffrages of their fellow-citizens, to stations of great pre-eminence and power, may find compensations for betraying their trust, which to any but minds actuated by superior virtue, may appear to exceed the proportion of interest they have in the common stock, and to overbalance the obligations of duty. Hence it is, that history furnishes us with so many mortifying examples of the prevalency of foreign corruption in republican governments. How much this contributed to the ruin of the ancient commonwealths, has been already disclosed. It is well known that the deputies of the United Provinces have, in various instances, been purchased by the emissaries of the neighbouring kingdoms. The earl of Chesterfield, if my memory serves me right, in a letter to his court, intimates, that his success in an important negotiation, must depend on his obtaining a major's commission for one of those deputies. And in Sweden, the rival parties were alternately bought by France and England, in so barefaced and notorious a manner, that it excited universal disgust in the nation; and was a principal cause that the most limited monarch in Europe, in a single day, without tumult, violence, or opposition, became one of the most absolute and uncontroled.

A circumstance which crowns the defects of the confederation, remains yet to be mentioned . . . the want of a judiciary power. Laws are a dead letter, without courts to expound and define their true meaning and operation. The treaties of the United States, to have any force at all, must be considered as part of the law of the land. Their true import, as far as respects individuals, must, like all other laws, be ascertained by judicial determinations. To produce uniformity in these determinations, they ought to be submitted, in the last resort, to one SUPREME TRIBUNAL. And this tribunal ought to be instituted under the same authority which forms the treaties themselves. These ingredients are both indispensable. If there is in each state a court of final jurisdiction, there may be as many different final determinations on the same point, as there are courts. There are endless diversities in the opinions of men. We often see not only different courts, but the judges of the same court, differing from each other. To avoid the confusion which would unavoidably result from the contradictory decisions of a number of independent judicatories, all nations have found it necessary to establish one tribunal paramount to the rest, possessing a general superintendence, and authorized to settle and declare in the last resort an uniform rule of civil justice.

This is the more necessary where the frame of the government is so compounded, that the laws of the whole are in danger of being contravened by the laws of the parts. In this case, if the particular tribunals are invested with a right of ultimate decision, besides the contradictions to be expected from difference of opinion, there will be much to fear from the bias of local views and prejudices, and from the interference of local regulations. As often as such an interference should happen, there would be reason to apprehend, that the provisions of the particular laws might be preferred to those of the general laws, from the deference with which men in office naturally look up to that authority to which they owe their official existence. The treaties of the United States, under the present constitution, are liable to the infractions of thirteen different legislatures, and as many different courts of final jurisdiction, acting under the authority of those legislatures. The faith, the reputation, the peace of the whole union, are thus continually at the mercy of the prejudices, the passions, and the interests of every member of which these are composed. Is it possible that foreign nations can either respect or confide in such a government? Is it possible that the people of America will longer consent to trust their honour, their happiness, their safety, on so precarious a foundation?

In this review of the confederation, I have confined myself to the exhibition of its most material defects; passing over those imperfections in its details, by which even a considerable part of the power intended to be conferred upon it, has been in a great measure rendered abortive. It must be by this time evident to all men of reflection, who are either free from erroneous prepossessions, or can divest themselves of them, that it is a system so radically vicious and unsound, as to admit not of amendment, but by an entire change in its leading features and characters.

The organization of congress is itself utterly improper for the exercise of those powers which are necessary to be deposited in the union. A single assembly may be a proper receptacle of those slender, or rather fettered authorities, which have been heretofore delegated to the federal head: but it would be inconsistent with all the principles of good government, to intrust it with those additional powers which even the moderate and more rational adversaries of the proposed constitution admit, ought to reside in the United States. If that plan should not be adopted; and if the necessity of union should be able to withstand the ambitious aims of those men, who may indulge magnificent schemes of personal aggrandizement from its dissolution; the probability would be, that we should run into the project of conferring supplementary powers upon congress, as they are now constituted. And either the machine, from the intrinsic feebleness of its structure, will moulder into pieces, in spite of our ill judged efforts to prop it; or, by successive augmentations of its force and energy, as necessity might prompt, we shall finally accumulate in a single body, all the most important prerogatives of sovereignty; and thus entail upon our posterity, one of the most execrable forms of government that human infatuation ever contrived. Thus we should create in reality that very tyranny, which the adversaries of the new constitution either are, or affect to be, solicitous to avert.

It has not a little contributed to the infirmities of the existing federal system, that it never had a ratification by the PEOPLE. Resting on no better foundation than the consent of the several legislatures, it has been exposed to frequent and intricate questions concerning the validity of its powers; and has, in some instances, given birth to the enormous doctrine of a right of legislative repeal. Owing its ratification to the law of a state, it has been contended, that the same authority might repeal the law by which it was ratified. However gross a heresy it may be to maintain, that a *party* to a *compact* has a right to revoke that *compact,* the doctrine itself has had respectable advocates. The possibility of a question of this nature, proves the necessity of laying the foundations of our national government deeper than in the mere sanction of delegated authority. The fabric of American empire ought to rest on the solid basis of THE CONSENT OF THE PEOPLE. The streams of national power ought to flow immediately from that pure original fountain of all legitimate authority.

PUBLIUS

No. 23

by Alexander Hamilton

The necessity of a government, at least equally energetic with the one proposed

The necessity of a constitution, at least equally energetic with the one proposed, to the preservation of the union, is the point, at the examination of which we are now arrived.

This inquiry will naturally divide itself into three branches. The objects to be provided for by a federal government: the quantity of power necessary to the accomplishment of those objects: the persons upon whom that power ought to operate. Its distribution and organization will more properly claim our attention under the succeeding head.

No. 23

The principal purposes to be answered by union, are these: the common defence of the members: the preservation of the public peace, as well against internal convulsions as external attacks; the regulation of commerce with other nations, and between the states; the superintendence of our intercourse, political and commercial, with foreign countries.

The authorities essential to the care of the common defence, are these: to raise armies; to build and equip fleets; to prescribe rules for the government of both; to direct their operations; to provide for their support. These powers ought to exist without limitation; because it is impossible to foresee or to define the extent and variety of national exigencies, and the correspondent extent and variety of the means which may be necessary to satisfy them. The circumstances that endanger the safety of nations are infinite; and for this reason, no constitutional shackles can wisely be imposed on the power to which the care of it is committed. This power ought to be co-extensive with all the possible combinations of such circumstances; and ought to be under the direction of the same councils which are appointed to preside over the common defence.

This is one of those truths which, to a correct and unprejudiced mind, carries its own evidence along with it; and may be obscured, but cannot be made plainer by argument or reasoning. It rests upon axioms, as simple as they are universal . . . the *means* ought to be proportioned to the *end;* the persons from whose agency the attainment of any *end* is expected, ought to possess the *means* by which it is to be attained.

Whether there ought to be a federal government intrusted with the care of the common defence, is a question, in the first instance, open to discussion; but the moment it is decided in the affirmative, it will follow, that, that government ought to be clothed with all the powers requisite to the complete execution of its trust. And unless it can be shown, that the circumstances which may affect the public safety, are reducible within certain determinate limits: unless the contrary of this position can be fairly and rationally disputed, it must be admitted as a necessary consequence, that there can be no limitation of that authority, which is to provide for the defence and protection of the community, in any matter essential to its efficacy; that is, in any matter essential to the *formation, direction,* or *support* of the NATIONAL FORCES.

Defective as the present confederation has been proved to be, this principle appears to have been fully recognized by the framers of it; though they have not made proper or adequate provision for its exercise. Congress have an unlimited discretion to make requisitions of men and money; to govern the army and navy; to direct their operations. As their requisitions are made constitutionally binding upon the states, who are in fact under the most solemn obligations to furnish the supplies required of them, the intention evidently was, that the United States should command whatever resources were by them judged requisite to the "common defence and general welfare." It was presumed, that a sense of their true interests, and a regard to the dictates of good faith, would be found sufficient pledges for the punctual performance of the duty of the members to the federal head.

The experiment has however demonstrated, that this expectation was ill founded and illusory; and the observations made under the last head will, I imagine, have sufficed to convince the impartial and discerning, that there is an absolute necessity for an entire change in the first principles of the system. That if we are in earnest about giving the union energy and duration, we must abandon the vain project of legislating upon the states in their collective capacities; we must extend the laws of the federal government to the individual citizens of America; we must discard the fallacious scheme of quotas and requisitions, as equally impracticable and unjust. The result from all this is, that the union ought to be invested with full power to levy troops; to build and equip fleets; and to raise the revenues which will be required for the formation and support of an army and navy, in the customary and ordinary modes practised in other governments.

If the circumstances of our country are such as to demand a compound, instead of a simple . . . a confederate, instead of a sole government, the essential point which will remain to be adjusted, will be to discriminate the OBJECTS, as far as it can be done, which shall appertain to the different provinces or departments of power: allowing to each the most ample authority for fulfilling THOSE which may be committed to its charge. Shall the union be constituted the guardian of the common safety? Are fleets, and armies, and revenues, necessary to this purpose? The government of the union must be empowered to pass all laws, and to make all regulations which have relation to them. The same must be the case in respect to commerce, and to every other matter to which its jurisdiction is permitted to extend. Is the administration of justice between the citizens of the same state, the proper department of the local governments? These must possess all the authorities which are connected with this object, and with every other that may be allotted to their particular cognizance and direction. Not to confer in each case a degree of power commensurate to the end, would be to violate the most obvious rules of prudence and propriety, and improvidently to trust the great interests of the nation to hands which are disabled from managing them with vigour and success.

Who so likely to make suitable provisions for the public defence, as that body to which the guardianship of the public safety is confided? Which, as the centre of information, will best understand the extent and urgency of the dangers that threaten; as the representative of the WHOLE, will feel itself most deeply interested in the preservation of every part; which, from the responsibility implied in the duty assigned to it, will be most sensibly impressed with the necessity of proper exactions; and which, by the extension of its authority throughout the states, can alone establish uniformity and concert in the plans and measures, by which the common safety is to be secured? Is there not a manifest inconsistency in devolving upon the federal government the care of the general defence, and leaving in the state governments the *effective* powers, by which it is to be provided for? Is not a want of cooperation the infallible consequence of such a system? And will not weakness, disorder, an undue distribution of the burthens and calamities of war, an unnecessary and intolerable increase of expense, be its natural and inevitable concomitants? Have we not had unequivocal experience of its effects in the course of the revolution which we have just achieved?

Every view we may take of the subject, as candid inquirers after truth, will serve to convince us, that it is both unwise and dangerous to deny the federal government an unconfined authority, in respect to all those objects which are intrusted to its management. It will indeed deserve the most vigilant and careful attention of the people, to see that it be modelled in such a manner as to admit of its being safely vested with the requisite powers. If any plan which has been, or may be, offered to our consideration, should not, upon a dispassionate inspection, be found to answer this description it ought to be rejected. A government, the constitution of which renders it unfit to be intrusted with all the powers which a free people *ought to delegate to any government,* would be an unsafe and improper depository of the NATIONAL INTERESTS. Wherever THESE can with propriety be confided, the coincident powers may safely accompany them. This is the true result of all just reasoning upon the subject. And the adversaries of the plan promulgated by the convention, would have given a better impression of their candour, if they had confined themselves to showing, that the internal structure of the proposed government was such as to render it unworthy of the confidence of the people. They ought not to have wandered into inflammatory declamations and unmeaning cavils, about the extent of the powers. The POWERS are not too extensive for the OBJECTS of federal administration, or, in other words, for the management of our NATIONAL INTERESTS; nor can any satisfactory argument be framed to show that they are chargeable with such an excess. If it be true, as has been insinuated by some of the writers on the other side, that the difficulty arises from the nature of the thing, and that the extent of the country will not permit us to form a government in which such ample powers can safely be reposed, it would prove that we ought to contract our views, and resort to the expedient of separate confederacies, which will move within more practicable spheres. For the absurdity must continually stare us in the face, of confiding to a government the direction of the most essential national concerns, without daring to trust it with the authorities which are indispensable to their proper and efficient management. Let us not attempt to reconcile contradictions, but firmly embrace a rational alternative.

I trust, however, that the impracticability of one general system cannot be shown. I am greatly mistaken, if any thing of weight has yet been advanced of this tendency; and I flatter myself, that the observations which have been made in the course of these papers, have served to place the reverse of that position in as clear a light as any matter, still in the womb of time and experience, is susceptible of. This, at all events, must be evident, that the very difficulty itself, drawn from the extent of the country, is the strongest argument in favour of an energetic government; for any other can certainly never preserve the union of so large an empire. If we embrace, as the standard of our political creed, the tenets of those who oppose the adoption of the proposed constitution, we cannot fail to verify the gloomy doctrines, which predict the impracticability of a national system, pervading the entire limits of the present confederacy.

PUBLIUS

No. 24

by Alexander Hamilton

The subject continued, with an answer to an objection concerning standing armies

To the powers proposed to be conferred upon the federal government, in respect to the creation and direction of the national forces, I have met with but one specific objection; which is, that proper provision has not been made against the existence of standing armies in time of peace: an objection which I shall now endeavour to show rests on weak and unsubstantial foundations.

It has indeed been brought forward in the most vague and general form, supported only by bold assertions, without the appearance of argument; without even the sanction of theoretical opinions, in contradiction to the practice of other free nations, and to the general sense of America, as expressed in most of the existing constitutions. The propriety of this remark will appear, the moment it is recollected that the objection under consideration turns upon a supposed necessity of restraining the LEGISLATIVE authority of the nation, in the article of military establishments; a principle unheard of, except in one or two of our state constitutions, and rejected in all the rest.

A stranger to our politics, who was to read our newspapers at the present juncture, without having previously inspected the plan reported by the convention, would be naturally led to one of two conclusions: either that it contained a positive injunction, that standing armies should be kept up in time of peace; or, that it vested in the EXECUTIVE the whole power of levying troops, without subjecting his discretion in any shape to the control of the legislature.

If he came afterwards to peruse the plan itself, he would be surprised to discover, that neither the one nor the other was the case; that the whole power of raising armies was lodged in the *legislature,* not in the *executive:* that this legislature was to be a popular body, consisting of the representatives of the people periodically elected; and that instead of the provision he had supposed in favour of standing armies, there was to be found in respect to this object, an important qualification even of the legislative discretion, in that clause which forbids the appropriation of money for the support of an army for any longer period than two years: a precaution which, upon a nearer view of it, will appear to be a great and real security against military establishments without evident necessity.

Disappointed in his first surmise, the person I have supposed would be apt to pursue his conjectures a little further. He would naturally say to himself, it is impossible that all this vehement and pathetic declamation can be without some colourable pretext. It must needs be that this people, so jealous of their liberties, have, in all the preceding models of the constitutions which they have established, inserted the most precise and rigid precautions on this point, the omission of which in the new plan, has given birth to all this apprehension and clamour.

If, under this impression, he proceeded to pass in review the several state constitutions, how great would be his disappointment to find that *two only* of them* contained an interdiction of standing armies in time of peace; that the other eleven had either observed a profound silence on the subject, or had in express terms admitted the right of the legislature to authorize their existence.

Still, however, he would be persuaded that there must be some plausible foundation, for the cry raised on this head. He would never be able to imag-

---

*This statement of the matter is taken from the printed collections of state constitutions. Pennsylvania and North Carolina are the two which contain the interdiction in these words: "As standing armies in time of peace are dangerous to liberty, THEY OUGHT NOT to be kept up." This is, in truth, rather a CAUTION than a PROHIBITION. New Hampshire, Massachusetts, Delaware and Maryland have, in each of their bills of rights, a clause to this effect: "Standing armies are dangerous to liberty, and ought not be raised or kept up WITHOUT THE CONSENT OF THE LEGISLATURE;" which is a formal admission of the authority of the legislature. New York has no bill of rights, and her constitution says not a word about the matter. No bills of rights appear annexed to the constitutions of the other states, and their constitutions are equally silent. I am told, however, that one or two states have bills of rights, which do not appear in this collection; but that those also recognize the right of the legislative authority in this respect.

ine, while any source of information remained unexplored, that it was nothing more than an experiment upon the public credulity, dictated either by a deliberate intention to deceive, or by the overflowings of a zeal too intemperate to be ingenuous. It would probably occur to him, that he would be likely to find the precautions he was in search of, in the primitive compact between the states. Here, at length, he would expect to meet with a solution of the enigma. No doubt, he would observe to himself, the existing confederation must contain the most explicit provisions against military establishments in time of peace; and a departure from this model in a favourite point, has occasioned the discontent, which appears to influence these political champions.

If he should now apply himself to a careful and critical survey of the articles of confederation, his astonishment would not only be increased, but would acquire a mixture of indignation, at the unexpected discovery, that these articles, instead of containing the prohibition he looked for, and though they had, with jealous circumspection, restricted the authority of the state legislatures in this particular, had not imposed a single restraint on that of the United States. If he happened to be a man of quick sensibility, or ardent temper, he could now no longer refrain from pronouncing these clamours to be the dishonest artifices of a sinister and unprincipled opposition to a plan, which ought at least to receive a fair and candid examination from all sincere lovers of their country! How else, he would say, could the authors of them have been tempted to vent such loud censures upon that plan, about a point, in which it seems to have conformed itself to the general sense of America as declared in its different forms of government, and in which it has even super-added a new and powerful guard unknown to any of them? If, on the contrary, he happened to be a man of calm and dispassionate feelings, he would indulge a sigh for the frailty of human nature, and would lament, that in a matter so interesting to the happiness of millions, the true merits of the question should be perplexed and obscured by expedients so unfriendly to an impartial and right determination. Even such a man could hardly forbear remarking, that a conduct of this kind, has too much the appearance of an intention to mislead the people by alarming their passions, rather than to convince them by arguments addressed to their understandings.

But however little this objection may be countenanced, even by precedents among ourselves, it may be satisfactory to take a nearer view of its intrinsic merits. From a close examination, it will appear, that restraints upon the discretion of the legislature, in respect to military establishments, would be improper to be imposed; and if imposed, from the necessities of society, would be unlikely to be observed.

Though a wide ocean separates the United States from Europe, yet there are various considerations that warn us against an excess of confidence or security. On one side of us, stretching far into our rear, are growing settlements subject to the dominion of Britain. On the other side, and extending to meet the British settlements, are colonies and establishments subject to the dominion of Spain. This situation, and the vicinity of the West India islands, belonging to these two powers, create between them, in respect to their American possessions, and in relation to us, a common interest. The savage tribes on our western frontier, ought to be regarded as our natural enemies; their natural allies: because they have most to fear from us, and most to hope from them. The improvements in the art of navigation, have, as to the facility of communication, rendered distant nations, in a great measure, neighbours. Britain and Spain, are among the principal maritime powers of Europe. A future concert of views between these nations, ought not to be regarded as improbable. The increasing remoteness of consanguinity, is every day diminishing the force of the family compact between France and Spain. And politicians have ever, with great reason, considered the ties of blood, as feeble and precarious links of political connexion. These circumstances, combined, admonish us not to be too sanguine in considering ourselves as entirely out of the reach of danger.

Previous to the revolution, and ever since the peace, there has been a constant necessity for keeping small garrisons on our western frontier. No person can doubt, that these will continue to be indispensable, if it should only be to guard against the ravages and depredations of the Indians. These garrisons must either be furnished by occasional detachments from the militia, or by permanent corps in the pay of the government. The first is impracticable; and if practicable, would be pernicious. The militia, in times of profound peace, would not long, if at all, submit to be dragged from their occupations and families, to perform that most disagreeable duty. And if they

No. 24

could be prevailed upon, or compelled to do it, the increased expense of a frequent rotation of service, and the loss of labour, and disconcertion of the industrious pursuits of individuals, would form conclusive objections to the scheme. It would be as burthensome and injurious to the public, as ruinous to private citizens. The latter resource of permanent corps in the pay of government, amounts to a standing army in time of peace; a small one, indeed, but not the less real for being small.

Here is a simple view of the subject, that shows us at once the impropriety of a constitutional interdiction of such establishments, and the necessity of leaving the matter to the discretion and prudence of the legislature.

In proportion to our increase in strength, it is probable, nay, it may be said certain, that Britain and Spain would augment their military establishments in our neighbourhood. If we should not be willing to be exposed, in a naked and defenceless condition, to their insults or encroachments, we should find it expedient to increase our frontier garrisons, in some ratio to the force by which our western settlements might be annoyed. There are, and will be, particular posts, the possession of which will include the command of large districts of territory, and facilitate future invasions of the remainder. It may be added, that some of those posts will be keys to the trade with the Indian nations. Can any man think it would be wise, to leave such posts in a situation to be at any instant seized by one or the other of two neighbouring and formidable powers? To act this part, would be to desert all the usual maxims of prudence and policy.

If we mean to be a commercial people, or even to be secure on our Atlantic side, we must endeavour, as soon as possible, to have a navy. To this purpose, there must be dock yards and arsenals; and, for the defence of these, fortifications, and probably garrisons. When a nation has become so powerful by sea, that it can protect its dock yards by its fleets, this supercedes the necessity of garrisons for that purpose; but where naval establishments are in their infancy, moderate garrisons will, in all likelihood, be found an indispensable security against descents for the destruction of the arsenals and dock yards, and sometimes of the fleet itself.

PUBLIUS

No. 25

by Alexander Hamilton

The subject continued, with the same view

It may perhaps be urged, that the objects enumerated in the preceding number ought to be provided by the state governments, under the direction of the union. But this would be an inversion of the primary principle of our political association; as it would in practice transfer the care of the common defence from the federal head to the individual members: a project oppressive to some states, dangerous to all, and baneful to the confederacy.

The territories of Britain, Spain, and of the Indian nations in our neighbourhood, do not border on particular states; but encircle the union from MAINE to GEORGIA. The danger, though in different degrees, is therefore common. And the means of guarding against it, ought, in like manner, to be the objects of common councils, and of a common treasury. It happens that some states, from local situation, are more directly exposed. NEW YORK is of this class. Upon the plan of separate provisions, New York would have to sustain the whole weight of the establishments requisite to her immediate safety, and to the mediate, or ultimate protection of her neighbours. This would neither be equitable as it respected New York, nor safe as it respected the other states. Various inconveniences would attend such a system. The states, to whose lot it might fall to support the necessary establishments, would be as little able as willing, for a considerable time to come, to bear the burthen of competent provisions. The security of all would thus be subjected to the parsimony, improvidence, or inability of a part. If, from the resources of such part becoming more abundant, its provisions should be proportionably enlarged, the other states would quickly take the alarm at seeing the whole military force of the union in the hands of two or three of its members; and those probably amongst the most powerful. They would each choose to have some counterpoise; and pretences could easily be contrived. In this situation, military establishments, nourished by mutual jealousy, would be apt to swell beyond their natural or proper size; and being at the separate disposal of the members, they would be engines for the abridgment, or demolition, of the national authority.

Reasons have been already given to induce a supposition, that the state governments will too naturally be prone to a rivalship with that of the union, the foundation of which will be the love of power; and that in any contest between the federal head and one of its members, the people will be most apt to unite with their local government. If, in addition to this immense advantage, the ambition of the members should be stimulated by the separate and independent possession of military forces, it would afford too strong a temptation, and too great facility to them to make enterprises upon, and finally to subvert, the constitutional authority of the union. On the other hand, the liberty of the people would be less safe in this state of things, than in that which left the national forces in the hands of the national government. As far as an army may be considered as a dangerous weapon of power, it had better be in those hands, of which the people are most likely to be jealous, than in those of which they are least likely to be so. For it is a truth which the experience of all ages has attested, that the people are commonly most in danger, when the means of injuring their rights are in the possession of those of whom they entertain the least suspicion.

The framers of the existing confederation, fully aware of the danger to the union from the separate possession of military forces by the states, have in express terms prohibited them from having either ships or troops, unless with the consent of congress. The truth is, that the existence of a federal government and military establishments, under state authority, are not less at variance with each other, than a due supply of the federal treasury and the system of quotas and requisitions.

There are other views besides those already presented, in which the impropriety of restraints on the discretion of the national legislature will be equally manifest. The design of the objection, which has been mentioned, is to preclude standing armies in time of peace; though we have never been informed how far it is desired the prohibition should extend: whether to raising armies, as well as to *keeping them up,* in a season of tranquillity, or not. If it be confined to the latter, it will have no precise signification, and it will be ineffectual for the purpose intended. When armies are once raised, what shall be denominated "keeping them up," contrary to the sense of the constitution? What time shall be requisite to ascertain the violation? Shall it be a week, a month, a year? Or shall we say, they may be continued as long as the danger which occasioned their being raised continues? This would be to admit that they might be kept up *in time of peace,* against threatening or impending danger; which would be at once to deviate from the literal meaning of the prohibition, and to introduce an extensive latitude of construction. Who shall judge of the continuance of the danger? This must undoubtedly be submitted to the national government, and the matter would then be brought to this issue, that the national government, to provide against apprehended danger, might, in the first instance, raise troops, and might afterwards keep them on foot, as long they supposed the peace or safety of the community was in any degree of jeopardy. It is easy to perceive, that a discretion so latitudinary as this, would afford ample room for eluding the force of the provision.

The utility of a provision of this kind, can only be vindicated on the hypothesis of a probability, at least possibility, of combination between the executive and legislature, in some scheme of usurpation. Should this at any time happen, how easy would it be to fabricate pretences of approaching danger? Indian hostilities, instigated by Spain or Britain, would always be at hand. Provocations to produce the desired appearances, might even be given to some foreign power, and appeased again by timely concessions. If we can reasonably presume such a combination to have been formed, and that the enterprise is warranted by a sufficient prospect of success; the army when once raised, from whatever cause, or on whatever pretext, may be applied to the execution of the project.

If to obviate this consequence, it should be resolved to extend the prohibition to the *raising* of armies in time of peace, the United States would then exhibit the most extraordinary spectacle, which the world has yet seen . . . that of a nation incapacitated by its constitution to prepare for defence, before it was actually invaded. As the ceremony of a formal denunciation of war has of late fallen into disuse, the presence of an enemy within our territories must be waited for, as the legal warrant to the government to begin its levies of men for the protection of the state. We must receive the blow, before we could even prepare to return it. All that kind of policy by which nations anticipate distant danger, and meet the gathering storm, must be abstained from, as contrary to the genuine maxims of a free government. We must expose our property and liberty to the mercy of foreign invaders, and invite them by our weakness, to seize the naked and defenceless prey, because we are afraid that rulers, created by our choice, dependent on our will might endanger that liberty, by an abuse of the means necessary to its preservation.

Here I expect we shall be told, that the militia of the country is its natural bulwark, and would at all times be equal to the national defence. This doctrine, in substance, had like to have lost us our independence. It cost millions to the United States, that might have been saved. The facts which from our own experience forbid a reliance of this kind, are too recent to permit us to be the dupes of such a suggestion. The steady operations of war against a regular and disciplined army, can only be successfully conducted by a force of the same kind. Considerations of economy, not less than of stability and vigour, confirm this position. The American militia, in the course of the late war, have, by their valour on numerous occasions, erected eternal monuments to their fame; but the bravest of them feel and know, that the liberty of their country could not have been established by their efforts alone, however great and valuable they were. War, like most other things, is a science to be acquired and perfected by diligence, by perseverance by time, and by practice.

All violent policy, as it is contrary to the natural and experienced course of human affairs, defeats itself. Pennsylvania at this instant affords an example of the truth of this remark. The bill of rights of that state declares, that standing armies are dangerous to liberty, and ought not to be kept up in time of peace. Pennsylvania, nevertheless, in a time of profound peace, from the existence of partial disorders in one or two of her counties, has resolved to raise a body of troops; and in all probability, will keep them up as long as there is any appearance of danger to the public peace. The conduct of Massachusetts affords a lesson on the same subject, though on different ground. That state (without waiting for the sanction of congress, as the articles of the confederation require) was compelled to raise troops to quell a domestic insurrection, and still keeps a corps in pay to prevent a revival of the spirit of revolt. The particular constitution of Massachusetts opposed no obstacle to the measure; but the instance is still of use to instruct us, that cases are likely to occur under our governments, as well as under those of other nations, which will sometimes render a military force in time of peace, essential to the security of the society, and that it is therefore improper, in this respect, to control the legislative discretion. It also teaches us, in its application to the United States, how little the rights of a feeble government are likely to be respected, even by its own constituents. And it teaches us, in addition to the rest, how unequal are parchment provisions, to a struggle with public necessity.

It was a fundamental maxim of the Lacedemonian commonwealth, that the post of admiral should not be conferred twice on the same person. The Peloponnesian confederates, having suffered a severe defeat at sea from the Atheniaus, demanded Lysander, who had before served with success in that capacity, to command the combined fleets. The Lacedemonians, to gratify their allies, and yet preserve the semblance of an adherence to their ancient institutions, had recourse to the flimsy subterfuge of investing Lysander with the real power of admiral, under the nominal title of vice admiral. This instance is selected from among a multitude that might be cited, to confirm the truth already advanced and illustrated by domestic examples; which is, that nations pay little regard to rules and maxims, calculated in their very nature to run counter to the necessities of society. Wise politicians will be cautious about fettering the government with restrictions, that cannot be observed; because they know, that every breach of the fundamental laws, though dictated by necessity, impairs that sacred reverence, which ought to be maintained in the breast of rulers towards the constitution of a country, and forms a precedent for other breaches, where the same plea of necessity does not exist at all, or is less urgent and palpable.

PUBLIUS

No. 26

by Alexander Hamilton

The subject continued with the same view

It was a thing hardly to have been expected, that in a popular revolution, the minds of men should stop at that happy mean which marks the salutary boundary between POWER and PRIVILEGE, and combines the energy of government with the security of private rights. A failure in this delicate and important point, is the great source of the inconveniences we experience; and if we are not cautious to avoid a repetition of the error, in our future attempts to rectify and ameliorate our system, we may travel from one chimerical project to another: we may try change after change; but we shall never be likely to make any material change for the better.

The idea of restraining the legislative authority, in the means for providing for the national defence, is one of those refinements, which owe their origin to a zeal for liberty more ardent than enlightened. We have seen, however, that it has not had thus far an extensive prevalency; that even in this country, where it made its first appearance, Pennsylvania and North Carolina are the only two states by which it has been in any degree patronized; and that all the others have refused to give it the least countenance. They wisely judged that confidence must be placed somewhere; that the necessity of doing it, is implied in the very act of delegating power; and that it is better to hazard the abuse of that confidence, than to embarrass the government and endanger the public safety, by impolitic restrictions on the legislative authority. The opponents of the proposed constitution, combat in this respect the general decision of America; and instead of being taught by experience the propriety of correcting any extremes into which we may have heretofore run, they appear disposed to conduct us into others still more dangerous, and more extravagant. As if the tone of government had been found too high, or too rigid, the doctrines they teach are calculated to induce us to depress, or to relax it, by expedients which, upon other occasions, have been condemned or forborne. It may be affirmed without the imputation of invective, that if the principles they inculcate on various points, could so far obtain as to become the popular creed, they would utterly unfit the people of this country for any species of government whatever. But a danger of this kind is not to be apprehended. The citizens of America have too much discernment to be argued into anarchy. And I am much mistaken, if experience has not wrought a deep and solemn conviction in the public mind, that greater energy of government is essential to the welfare and prosperity of the community.

It may not be amiss in this place, concisely to remark the origin and progress of the idea, which aims at the exclusion of military establishments in time of peace. Though in speculative minds, it may arise from a contemplation of the nature and tendency of such institutions, fortified by the events that have happened in other ages and countries; yet, as a national sentiment, it must be traced to those habits of thinking which we derive from the nation, from which the inhabitants of these states have in general sprung.

In England, for a long time after the Norman conquest, the authority of the monarch was almost unlimited. Inroads were gradually made upon the prerogative, in favour of liberty, first by the barons, and afterwards by the people, till the greatest part of its most formidable pretensions became extinct. But it was not till the revolution in 1688, which elevated the prince of Orange to the throne of Great Britain, that English liberty was completely triumphant. As incident to the undefined power of making war, an acknowledged prerogative of the crown, Charles II had, by his own authority, kept on foot in time of peace a body of 5,000 regular troops. And this number James II, increased to 30,000; who were paid out of his civil list. At the revolution, to abolish the exercise of so dangerous an authority, it became an article of the bill of rights then framed, that "raising or keeping a standing army within the kingdom in time of peace, *unless with the consent of parliament,* was against law."

In that kingdom, when the pulse of liberty was at its highest pitch, no security against the danger of standing armies was thought requisite, beyond a prohibition of their being raised or kept up by the mere authority of the executive magistrate. The patriots, who effected that memorable revolution, were too temperate, and too well informed, to think of any restraint on the legislative discretion. They were aware, that a certain number of troops for guards and garrisons were indispensable; that no precise bounds could be set to the national exigencies; that a power equal to every possible contingency must exist somewhere in the government; and that when they referred the exercise of that power to the judgment of the legislature, they had arrived at the ultimate point of precaution, which was reconcileable with the safety of the community.

From the same source, the people of America may be said to have derived an hereditary impression of danger to liberty, from standing armies in time of peace. The circumstances of a revolution quickened the public sensibility on every point connected with the security of popular rights, and in some instances raised the warmth of our zeal beyond the degree, which consisted with the due temperature of the body politic. The attempts of two of the states, to restrict the authority of the legislature in the article of military establishments, are of the number of these instances. The principles which had taught us to be jealous of the power of an hereditary monarch, were, by an injudicious excess, extended to the representatives of the people in their popular assemblies. Even in some of the states, where this error was not adopted, we find unnecessary declarations, that standing armies ought not to be kept up, in time of peace, *without the consent of the legislature.* I call them unnecessary, because the reason which had introduced a similar provision into the English bill of rights, is not applicable to any of the state constitutions. The power of raising armies at all, under those constitutions, can by no construction be deemed to reside any where else, than in the legislatures themselves; and it was superfluous, if not absurd, to declare, that a matter should not be done without the consent of a body, which alone had the power of doing it. Accordingly, in some of those constitutions, and among others, in that of the state of New York, which has been justly celebrated, both in Europe and America, as one of the best of the forms of government established in this country, there is a total silence upon the subject.

It is remarkable, that even in the two states, which seem to have meditated an interdiction of military establishments in time of peace, the mode of expression made use of is rather monitory, than prohibitory. It is not said, that standing armies *shall not be* kept up, but that they *ought not* to be kept up in time of peace. This ambiguity of terms appears to have been the result of a conflict between jealousy and conviction; between the desire of excluding such establishments at all events, and the persuasion that an absolute exclusion would be unwise and unsafe.

Can it be doubted that such a provision, whenever the situation of public affairs was understood to require a departure from it, would be interpreted by the legislature into a mere admonition, and would be made to yield to the actual or supposed necessities of the state? Let the fact already mentioned with respect to Pennsylvania, decide. What then, it may be asked, is the use of such a provision, if it cease to operate, the moment there is an inclination to disregard it?

Let us examine whether there be any comparison, in point of efficacy, between the provision alluded to, and that which is contained in the new constitution, for restraining the appropriations of money for military purposes to the period of two years. The former, by aiming at too much, is calculated to effect nothing: the latter, by steering clear of an imprudent extreme, and by being perfectly compatible with a proper provision for the exigencies of the nation, will have a salutary and powerful operation.

The legislature of the United States will be *obliged,* by this provision, once at least in every two years, to deliberate upon the propriety of keeping a military force on foot; to come to a new resolution on the point; and to declare their sense of the matter, by a formal vote in the face of their constituents. They are not at *liberty* to vest in the executive department, permanent funds for the support of an army; if they were even incautious enough to be willing to repose in it so improper a confidence. As the spirit of party, in different degrees, must be expected to infect all political bodies, there will be, no doubt, persons in the national legislature willing enough to arraign the measures, and criminate the views of the majority. The provision for the support of a military force, will always be a favourable topic for declamation. As often as the question comes forward, the public attention will be roused and attracted to the subject, by the party in opposition: and if the majority should be really disposed to exceed the proper limits, the community will be warned of the danger, and will have an opportunity of taking measures to guard against it. Independent of parties in the national legislature itself, as often as the period of discussion arrived, the state legislatures, who will always be not only vigilant, but suspicious and jealous guardians of the rights of the citizens, against encroachments from the federal government, will constantly have their attention awake to the conduct of the national rulers, and will be ready enough, if any thing improper appears, to sound the alarm to the people, and not only to be the VOICE, but if necessary, the ARM of their discontent.

Schemes to subvert the liberties of a great community, *require time to mature them for execution.* An army, so large as seriously to menace those liberties, could only be formed by progressive augmentations; which would suppose, not merely a temporary combination between the legislature and executive, but a continued conspiracy for a series of time. Is it probable that such a combination would exist at all? Is it probable that it would be persevered in, and transmitted through all the successive variations in the representative body, which biennial elections would naturally produce in both houses? Is it presumable, that every man, the instant he took his seat in the national senate or house of representatives, would commence a traitor to his constituents and to his country? Can it be supposed, that there would not be found one man, discerning enough to detect so atrocious a conspiracy, or bold or honest enough to apprize his constituents of their danger? If such presumptions can fairly be made, there ought at once to be an end of all delegated authority. The people should resolve to recal all the powers they have heretofore parted with; and to divide themselves into as many states as there are counties, in order that they may be able to manage their own concerns in person.

If such suppositions could even be reasonably made, still the concealment of the design, for any duration, would be impracticable. It would be announced, by the very circumstance of augmenting the army to so great an extent, in time of profound peace. What colourable reason could be assigned, in a country so situated, for such vast augmentations of the military force? It is impossible that the people could be long deceived; and the destruction of the project, and of the projectors, would quickly follow the discovery.

It has been said, that the provision which limits the appropriation of money for the support of an army to the period of two years, would be unavailing; because the executive, when once possessed of a force large enough to awe the people into submission, would find resources in that very force, sufficient to enable him to dispense with supplies from the votes of the legislature. But the question again recurs: upon what pretence could he be put in possession of a force of that magnitude in time of peace? If we suppose it to have been created in consequence of some domestic insurrection or foreign war, then it becomes a case not within the principle of the objection; for this is levelled against the power of keeping up troops in time of peace. Few persons will be so visionary, as seriously to contend that military forces ought not to be raised to quell a rebellion, or resist an invasion; and if the defence of the community, under such circumstances, should make it necessary to have an army, so numerous as to hazard its liberty, this is one of those calamities for which there is neither preventative nor cure. It cannot be provided against by any possible form of government: it might even result from a simple league offensive and defensive; if it should ever be necessary for the confederates or allies, to form an army for common defence.

But it is an evil infinitely less likely to attend us in an united, than in a disunited state; nay, it may be safely asserted, that it is an evil altogether unlikely to attend us in the latter situation. It is not easy to conceive a possibility, that dangers so formidable can assail the whole union, as to demand a force considerable enough to place our liberties in the least jeopardy; especially if we take into view the aid to be derived from the militia, which ought always to be counted upon as a valuable and powerful auxiliary. But in a state of disunion, as has been fully shown in another place, the contrary of this supposition would become not only probable, but almost unavoidable.

PUBLIUS

No. 27

by Alexander Hamilton

The subject continued, with the same view

It has been urged, in different shapes, that a constitution of the kind proposed by the convention, cannot operate without the aid of a military force to execute its laws. This, however, like most other things that have been alleged on that side, rests on mere general assertion, unsupported by any precise or intelligible designation of the reasons upon which it is founded. As far as I have been able to divine the latent meaning of the objectors, it seems to originate in a pre-supposition, that the people will be disinclined to the exercise of federal authority, in any matter of an internal nature. Wa[i]ving any exception that might be taken to the inaccuracy, or inexplicitness, of the distinction between internal and external, let us inquire what ground there is to pre-suppose that disinclination in the people. Unless we presume, at the same time, that the powers of the general government will be worse administered than those of the state governments, there seems to be no room for the presumption of ill will, disaffection, or opposition in the people. I believe it may be laid down as a general rule, that their confidence in, and their obedience to, a government, will commonly be proportioned to the goodness or badness of its administration. It must be admitted, that there are exceptions to this rule; but these exceptions depend so entirely on accidental causes, that they cannot be considered as having any relation to the intrinsic merits or demerits of a constitution. These can only be judged of by general principles and maxims.

Various reasons have been suggested, in the course of these papers, to induce a probability, that the general government will be better administered than the particular governments: the principal of which are, that the extension of the spheres of election will present a greater option, or latitude of choice, to the people; that, through the medium of the state legislatures, who are select bodies of men, and who are to appoint the members of the national senate, there is reason to expect, that this branch will generally be composed with peculiar care and judgment; that these circumstances promise greater knowledge, and more comprehensive information, in the national councils; and that, on account of the extent of the country from which will be drawn those to whose direction they will be committed, they will be less apt to be tainted by the spirit of faction, and more out of the reach of those occasional ill humours, or temporary prejudices and propensities, which, in smaller societies, frequently contaminate the public deliberations, beget injustice and oppression towards a part of the community, and engender schemes, which, though they gratify a momentary inclination or desire, terminate in general distress, dissatisfaction, and disgust. Several additional reasons of considerable force, will occur, to fortify that probability, when we come to survey, with a more critical eye, the interior structure of the edifice which we are invited to erect. It will be sufficient here to remark, that until satisfactory reasons can be assigned to justify an opinion, that the federal government is likely to be administered in such a manner as to render it odious or contemptible to the people, there can be no reasonable foundation for the supposition, that the laws of the union will meet with any greater obstruction from them, or will stand in need of any other methods to enforce their execution, than the laws of the particular members.

The hope of impunity, is a strong incitement to sedition: the dread of punishment, a proportionably strong discouragement to it. Will not the government of the union, which, if possessed of a due degree of power, can call to its aid the collective resources of the whole confederacy, be more likely to repress the *former* sentiment, and to inspire the *latter,* than that of a single state, which can only command the resources within itself? A turbulent faction in a state, may easily suppose itself able to contend with the friends to the government in that state; but it can hardly be so infatuated, as to imagine itself equal to the combined efforts of the union. If this reflection be just, there is less danger of resistance from irregular combinations of individuals, to the authority of the confederacy, than to that of a single member.

I will, in the first place, hazard an observation, which will not be the less just, because to some it may appear new; which is, that the more the operations of the national authority are intermingled in the ordinary exercise of government; the more the citizens are accustomed to meet with it in the common occurrences of their political life; the more it is familiarized to their sight, and to their feelings; the further it enters into those objects, which touch the most sensible chords, and put in motion the most active springs of the human heart; . . . the greater will be the probability, that it will conciliate the respect and attachment of the community. Man is very much a creature of habit. A thing that rarely strikes his senses, will have but a transient influence upon his mind. A government continually at a distance and out of sight, can hardly be expected to interest the sensations of the people. The inference is, that the authority of the union, and the affections of the citizens towards it, will be strengthened, rather than weakened, by its extension to what are called matters of internal concern; and that it will have less occasion to recur to force, in proportion to the familiarity and comprehensiveness of its agency. The more it circulates through those channels and currents, in which the passions of mankind naturally flow, the less will it require the aid of the violent and perilous expedients of compulsion.

One thing, at all events, must be evident, that a government like the one proposed, would bid much fairer to avoid the necessity of using force, than the species of league contended for by most of its opponents; the authority of which should only operate upon the states in their political or collective capacities. It has been shown, that in such a confederacy there can be no sanction for the laws but force; that frequent delinquencies in the members, are the natural offspring of the very frame of the government; and that as often as these happen, they can only be redressed, if at all, by war and violence.

The plan reported by the convention, by extending the authority of the federal head to the individual citizens of the several states, will enable the government to employ the ordinary magistracy of each, in the execution of its laws. It is easy to perceive, that this will tend to destroy, in the common apprehension, all distinction between the sources from which they might proceed; and will give the federal government the same advantage for securing a due obedience to its authority, which is enjoyed by the government of each state; in addition to the influence on public opinion, which will result from the important consideration, of its having power to call to its assistance and support the resources of the whole union. It merits particular attention in this place, that the laws of the confederacy, as to the *enumerated* and *legitimate* objects of its jurisdiction, will become the SUPREME LAW of the land; to the observance of which, all officers, legislative, executive, and judicial, in each state, will be bound by the sanctity of an oath. Thus the legislatures, courts, and magistrates, of the respective members, will be incorporated into the operations of the national government, *as far as its just and constitutional authority extends;* and will be rendered auxiliary to the enforcement of its laws.* Any man, who will pursue, by his own reflections, the consequences of this situation, will perceive, that if its powers are administered with a common share of prudence, there is good ground to calculate upon a regular and peaceable execution of the laws of the union. If we will arbitrarily suppose the contrary, we may deduce any inferences we please from the supposition; for it is certainly possible, by an injudicious exercise of the authorities of the best government that ever was, or ever can be instituted, to provoke and precipitate the people into the wildest excesses. But though the adversaries of the proposed constitution should presume, that the national rulers would be insensible to the motives of public good, or to the obligations of duty; I would still ask them, how the interests of ambition, or the views of encroachment, can be promoted by such a conduct?

PUBLIUS

---

*The sophistry which has been employed, to show that this will tend to the destruction of the state governments will, in its proper place, be fully detected.

No. 28

by Alexander Hamilton

The same subject continued

That there may happen cases, in which the national government may be under the necessity of resorting to force, cannot be denied. Our own experience has corroborated the lessons taught by the examples of other nations; that emergencies of this sort will sometimes exist in all societies, however constituted; that seditions and insurrections are, unhappily, maladies as inseparable from the body politic, as tumours and eruptions from the natural body; that the idea of governing at all times by the simple force of law, (which we have been told is the only admissible principle of republican government) has no place but in the reverie of those political doctors, whose sagacity disdains the admonitions of experimental instruction.

Should such emergencies at any time happen under the national government, there could be no remedy but force. The means to be employed, must be proportioned to the extent of the mischief. If it should be a slight commotion in a small part of a state, the militia of the residue would be adequate to its suppression: and the natural presumption is, that they would be ready to do their duty. An insurrection, whatever may be its immediate cause, eventually endangers all government. Regard to the public peace, if not to the rights of the union, would engage the citizens, to whom the contagion had not communicated itself, to oppose the insurgents: and if the general government should be found in practice conducive to the prosperity and felicity of the people, it were irrational to believe that they would be disinclined to its support.

If, on the contrary, the insurrection should pervade a whole state, or a principal part of it, the employment of a different kind of force might become unavoidable. It appears that Massachusetts found it necessary to raise troops for suppressing the disorders within that state; that Pennsylvania, from the mere apprehension of commotions among a part of her citizens, has thought proper to have recourse to the same measure. Suppose the state of New York had been inclined to re-establish her lost jurisdiction over the inhabitants of Vermont; could she have hoped for success in such an enterprise, from the efforts of the militia alone? Would she not have been compelled to raise, and to maintain, a more regular force for the execution of her design? If it must then be admitted, that the necessity of recurring to a force different from the militia, in cases of this extraordinary nature, is applicable to the state governments themselves, why should the possibility, that the national government might be under a like necessity in similar extremities, be made an objection to its existence? Is it not surprising that men, who declare an attachment to the union in the abstract, should urge, as an objection to the proposed constitution, what applies with ten-fold weight to the plan for which they contend; and what, as far as it has any foundation in truth, is an inevitable consequence of civil society upon an enlarged scale? Who would not prefer that possibility, to the unceasing agitations, and frequent revolutions, which are the continual scourges of petty republics?

Let us pursue this examination in another light. Suppose, in lieu of one general system, two or three, or even four confederacies were to be formed, would not the same difficulty oppose itself to the operations of either of these confederacies? Would not each of them be exposed to the same casualties; and, when these happened, be obliged to have recourse to the same expedients for upholding its authority, which are objected to a government for all the states? Would the militia, in this supposition, be more ready or more able to support the federal authority, than in the case of a general union? All candid and intelligent men must, upon due consideration, acknowledge, that the principle of the objection is equally applicable to either of the two cases; and that whether we have one government for all the states, or different governments for different parcels of them, or as many unconnected governments as there are states, there might sometimes be a necessity to make use of a force constituted differently from the militia, to preserve the peace of the community, and to maintain the just authority of the laws against those violent invasions of them, which amount to insurrections and rebellions.

Independent of all other reasonings upon the subject, it is a full answer to those who require a more peremptory provision against military establishments in time of peace, to say, that the whole power of the proposed government is to be in the hands of the representatives of the people. This is the essential, and, after all, the only efficacious security for the rights and privileges of the people, which is attainable in civil society.*

If the representatives of the people betray their constituents, there is then no resource left but in the exertion of that original right of self-defence, which is paramount to all positive forms of government; and which, against the usurpation of the national rulers, may be exerted with an infinitely better prospect of success, than against those of the rulers of an individual state. In a single state, if the persons intrusted with supreme power become usurpers, the different parcels, subdivisions, or districts, of which it consists, having no distinct government in each, can take no regular measures for defence. The citizens must rush tumultuously to arms, without concert, without system, without resource; except in their courage and despair. The usurpers, clothed with the forms of legal authority, can too often crush the opposition in embryo. The smaller the extent of territory, the more difficult will it be for the people to form a regular, or systematic plan of opposition; and the more easy will it be to defeat their early efforts. Intelligence can be more speedily obtained of their preparations and movements; and the military force in the possession of the usurpers, can be more rapidly directed against the part where the opposition has begun. In this situation, there must be a peculiar coincidence of circumstances to ensure success to the popular resistance.

The obstacles to usurpation, and the facilities of resistance, increase with the increased extent of the state: provided the citizens understand their rights, and are disposed to defend them. The natural strength of the people in a large community, in proportion to the artificial strength of the government, is greater than in a small; and of course more competent to a struggle with the attempts of the government to establish a tyranny. But in a confederacy, the people, without exaggeration, may be said to be entirely the masters of their own fate. Power being almost always the rival of power, the general government will, at all times, stand ready to check the usurpations of the state governments; and these will have the same disposition towards the general government. The people, by throwing themselves into either scale,

---

*Its full efficacy will be examined hereafter.

No. 28

will infallibly make it preponderate. If their rights are invaded by either, they can make use of the other, as the instrument of redress. How wise will it be in them, by cherishing the union, to preserve to themselves an advantage which can never be too highly prized!

It may safely be received as an axiom in our political system, that the state governments will, in all possible contingencies, afford complete security against invasions of the public liberty by the national authority. Projects of usurpation cannot be masked under pretences so likely to escape the penetration of select bodies of men, as of the people at large. The legislatures will have better means of information; they can discover the danger at a distance; and possessing all the organs of civil power, and the confidence of the people, they can at once adopt a regular plan of opposition, in which they can combine all the resources of the community. They can readily communicate with each other in the different states; and unite their common forces, for the protection of their common liberty.

The great extent of the country is a further security. We have already experienced its utility against the attacks of a foreign enemy. And it would have precisely the same effect against the enterprises of ambitious rulers in the national councils. If the federal army should be able to quell the resistance of one state, the distant states would have it in their power to make head with fresh forces. The advantages obtained in one place must be abandoned, to subdue the opposition in others; and the moment the part which had been reduced to submission was left to itself, its efforts would be renewed, and its resistance revive.

We should recollect, that the extent of the military force must, at all events, be regulated by the resources of the country. For a long time to come, it will not be possible to maintain a large army; and as the means of doing this, increase the population, and the natural strength of the community will proportionably increase. When will the time arrive, that the federal government can raise and maintain an army capable of creating a despotism over the great body of the people of an immense empire, who are in a situation, through the medium of their state governments, to take measures for their own defence, with all the celerity, regularity, and system, of independent nations? The apprehension may be considered as a disease, for which there can be found no cure in the resources of argument and reasoning.

PUBLIUS

No. 29

by Alexander Hamilton

Concerning the militia

The power of regulating the militia, and of commanding its services in times of insurrection and invasion, are natural incidents to the duties of superintending the common defence, and of watching over the internal peace of the confederacy.

It requires no skill in the science of war to discern, that uniformity in the organization and discipline of the militia, would be attended with the most beneficial effects, whenever they were called into service for the public defence. It would enable them to discharge the duties of the camp, and of the field, with mutual intelligence and concert . . . an advantage of peculiar moment in the operations of an army; and it would fit them much sooner to acquire the degree of proficiency in military functions, which would be essential to their usefulness. This desirable uniformity can only be accomplished, by confiding the regulation of the militia to the direction of the national authority. It is, therefore, with the most evident propriety, that the plan of the convention proposes to empower the union "to provide for organizing, arming and disciplining the militia, and for governing such part of them as may be employed in the service of the United States, *reserving to the states respectively the appointment of the officers, and the authority of training the militia according to the discipline prescribed by congress.*"

Of the different grounds which have been taken in opposition to this plan, there is none that was so little to have been expected, or is so untenable in itself, as the one from which this particular provision has been attacked. If a well regulated militia be the most natural defence of a free country, it ought certainly to be under the regulation, and at the disposal of that body, which is constituted the guardian of the national security. If standing armies are dangerous to liberty, an efficacious power over the militia, in the same body, ought, as far as possible, to take away the inducement and the pretext, to such unfriendly institutions. If the federal government can command the aid of the militia in those emergencies, which call for the military arm in support of the civil magistrate, it can the better dispense with the employment of a different kind of force. If it cannot avail itself of the former, it will be obliged to recur to the latter. To render an army unnecessary, will be a more certain method of preventing its existence, than a thousand prohibitions upon paper.

In order to cast an odium upon the power of calling forth the militia to execute the laws of the union, it has been remarked, that there is no where any provision in the proposed constitution for requiring the aid of the POSSE COMITATUS, to assist the magistrate in the execution of his duty; whence it has been inferred, that military force was intended to be his only auxiliary. There is a striking incoherence in the objections which have appeared, and sometimes even from the same quarter, not much calculated to inspire a very favourable opinion of the sincerity or fair dealing of their authors. The same persons who tell us in one breath, that the powers of the federal government will be despotic and unlimited, inform us in the next, that it has not authority sufficient even to call out the POSSE COMITATUS. The latter, fortunately, is as much short of the truth, as the former exceeds it. It would be as absurd to doubt, that a right to pass all laws *necessary* and *proper* to execute its declared powers, would include that of requiring the assistance of the citizens to the officers who may be intrusted with the execution of those laws; as it would be to believe, that a right to enact laws necessary and proper for the imposition and collection of taxes, would involve that of varying the rules of descent, and of the alienation of landed property, or of abolishing the trial by jury in cases relating to it. It being therefore evident, that the supposition of a want of power to require the aid of the POSSE COMITATUS is entirely destitute of colour, it will follow, that the conclusion which has been drawn from it, in its application to the authority of the federal government over the militia, is as uncandid, as it is illogical. What reason could there be to infer, that force was intended to be the sole instrument of authority, merely because there is a power to make use of it when necessary? What shall we think of the motives which could induce men of sense to reason in this extraordinary manner? How shall we prevent a conflict between charity and conviction?

By a curious refinement upon the spirit of republican jealousy, we are even taught to apprehend danger from the militia itself, in the hands of the federal government. It is observed, that select corps may be formed, composed of the young and the ardent, who may be rendered subservient to the views of arbitrary power. What plan for the regulation of the militia may be pursued by the national government, is impossible to be foreseen. But so far from viewing the matter in the same light with those who object to select corps as dangerous, were the constition ratified, and were I to deliver my sentiments to a member of the federal legislature on the subject of a militia establishment, I should hold to him in substance the following discourse:

"The project of disciplining all the militia of the United States, is as futile as it would be injurious, if it were capable of being carried into execution. A tolerable expertness in military movements, is a business that requires time and practice. It is not a day, nor a week, nor even a month, that will suffice for the attainment of it. To oblige the great body of the yeomanry, and of the other classes of the citizens, to be under arms for the purpose of going through military exercises and evolutions, as often as might be necessary to acquire the degree of perfection which would entitle them to the character of a well regulated militia, would be a real grievance to the people, and a serious public inconvenience and loss. It would form an annual deduction from the productive labour of the country, to an amount, which, calculating upon the present numbers of the people, would not fall far short of a million of pounds. To attempt a thing which would abridge the mass of labour and industry to so considerable an extent, would be unwise; and the experiment, if made, could not succeed, because it would not long be endured. Little more can reasonably be aimed at, with respect to the people at large, than to have them properly armed and equipped; and in order to see that this be not neglected, it will be necessary to assemble them once or twice in the course of a year.

"But, though the scheme of disciplining the whole nation must be abandoned as mischievous or impracticable; yet it is a matter of the utmost importance, that a well digested plan should, as soon as possible, be adopted for the proper establishment of the militia. The attention of the government ought particularly to be directed to the formation of a select corps of moderate size, upon such principles as will really fit it for service in case of need. By thus circumscribing the plan, it will be possible to have an excellent body of well trained militia, ready to take the field whenever the defence of the state shall require it. This will not only lessen the call for military establishments; but if circumstances should at any time oblige the government to form an army of any magnitude, that army can never be formidable to the liberties of the people, while there is a large body of citizens, little, if at all, inferior to them in discipline and the use of arms, who stand ready to defend their own rights, and those of their fellow citizens. This appears to me the only substitute that can be devised for a standing army; and the best possible security against it, if it should exist."

Thus differently from the adversaries of the proposed constitution should I reason on the same subject; deducing arguments of safety from the very sources which they represent as fraught with danger and perdition. But how the national legislature may reason on the point, is a thing which neither they nor I can foresee.

There is something so far fetched, and so extravagant, in the idea of danger to liberty from the militia, that one is at a loss whether to treat it with gravity or with raillery; whether to consider it as a mere trial of skill, like the paradoxes of rhetoricians; as a disingenuous artifice, to instil prejudices at any price; or as the serious offspring of political fanaticism. Where, in the name of common sense, are our fears to end, if we may not trust our sons, our brothers, our neighbours, our fellow citizens? What shadow of danger can there be from men, who are daily mingling with the rest of their countrymen; and who participate with them in the same feelings, sentiments, habits, and interests? What reasonable cause of apprehension can be inferred from a power in the union to prescribe regulations for the militia, and to command its services when necessary; while the particular states are to have the *sole and exclusive appointment of the officers?* If it were possible seriously to indulge a jealousy of the militia, upon any conceivable establishment under the federal government, the circumstance of the officers being in the appointment of the states, ought at once to extinguish it. There can be no doubt, that this circumstance will always secure to them a preponderating influence over the militia.

In reading many of the publications against the constitution, a man is apt to imagine that he is perusing some ill written tale or romance; which, instead of natural and agreeable images, exhibits to the mind nothing but frightful and distorted shapes. . . .

> "*Gorgons, Hydras, and Chimeras dire;*"

discolouring and disfiguring whatever it represents, and transforming every thing it touches into a monster.

A sample of this is to be observed in the exaggerated and improbable suggestions which have taken place respecting the power of calling for the services of the militia. That of New Hampshire is to be marched to Georgia, of Georgia to New Hampshire, of New York to Kentucky, and of Kentucky to Lake Champlain. Nay, the debts due to the French and Dutch, are to be paid in militia men, instead of Louis d'ors and ducats. At one moment, there is to be a large army to lay prostrate the liberties of the people; at another moment, the militia of Virginia are to be dragged from their homes, five or six hundred miles, to tame the republican contumacy of Massachusetts; and that of Massachusetts is to be transported an equal distance, to subdue the refractory haughtiness of the aristocratic Virginians. Do the persons, who rave at this rate, imagine, that their art or their eloquence can impose any conceits or absurdities upon the people of America for infallible truths?

If there should be an army to be made use of as the engine of despotism, what need of the militia? If there should be no army, whither would the militia, irritated at being required to undertake a distant and distressing expedition, for the purpose of rivetting the chains of slavery upon a part of their countrymen, direct their course, but to the seat of the tyrants, who had meditated so foolish, as well as so wicked a project; to crush them in their imagined entrenchments of power, and make them an example of the just vengeance of an abused and incensed people? Is this the way in which usurpers stride to dominion over a numerous and enlightened nation? Do they begin by exciting the detestation of the very instruments of their intended usurpations? Do they usually commence their career by wanton and disgustful acts of power, calculated to answer no end, but to draw upon themselves universal hatred and execration? Are suppositions of this sort, the sober admonitions of discerning patriots to a discerning people? Or are they the inflammatory ravings of chagrined incendiaries, or distempered enthusiasts? If we were even to suppose the national rulers actuated by the most ungovernable ambition, it is impossible to believe that they would employ such preposterous means to accomplish their designs.

In times of insurrection, or invasion, it would be natural and proper, that the militia of a neighbouring state should be marched into another, to resist a common enemy, or to guard the republic against the violences of faction or sedition. This was frequently the case, in respect to the first object, in the course of the late war; and this mutual succour is, indeed, a principal end of our political association. If the power of affording it be placed under the direction of the union, there will be no danger of a supine and listless inattention to the dangers of a neighbour, till its near approach had superadded the incitements of self-preservation, to the too feeble impulses of duty and sympathy.

PUBLIUS

No. 30

by Alexander Hamilton

Concerning taxation

It has been already observed, that the federal government ought to possess the power of providing for the support of the national forces; in which proposition was intended to be included the expense of raising troops, of building and equipping fleets, and all other expenses in any wise connected with military arrangements and operations. But these are not the only objects to which the jurisdiction of the union, in respect to revenue, must necessarily be empowered to extend. It must embrace a provision for the support of the national civil list; for the payment of the national debts contracted, or that may be contracted; and, in general, for all those matters which will call for disbursements out of the national treasury. The conclusion is, that there must be interwoven in the frame of the government, a general power of taxation in one shape or another.

Money is with propriety considered as the vital principle of the body politic; as that which sustains its life and motion, and enables it to perform its most essential functions. A complete power, therefore, to procure a regular and adequate supply of revenue, as far as the resources of the community will permit, may be regarded as an indispensable ingredient in every constitution. From a deficiency in this particular, one of two evils must ensue; either the people must be subjected to continual plunder, as a substitute for a more eligible mode of supplying the public wants, or the government must sink into a fatal atrophy, and in a short course of time perish.

In the Ottoman or Turkish empire, the sovereign, though in other respects absolute master of the lives and fortunes of his subjects, has no right to impose a new tax. The consequence is, that he permits the bashaws or governors of provinces to pillage the people at discretion; and, in turn, squeezes out of them the sums of which he stands in need, to satisfy his own exigencies, and those of the state. In America, from a like cause, the government of the union has gradually dwindled into a state of decay, approaching nearly to annihilation. Who can doubt, that the happiness of the people in both countries would be promoted by competent authorities in the proper hands, to provide the revenues which the necessities of the public might require?

The present confederation, feeble as it is, intended to repose in the United States an unlimited power of providing for the pecuniary wants of the union. But proceeding upon an erroneous principle, it has been done in such a manner as entirely to have frustrated the intention. Congress, by the articles which compose that compact (as has been already stated) are authorized to ascertain and call for any sums of money necessary, in their judgment, to the service of the United States; and their requisitions, if conformable to the rule of apportionment, are, in every constitutional sense, obligatory upon the states. These have no right to question the propriety of the demand; no discretion beyond that of devising the ways and means of furnishing the sums demanded. But though this be strictly and truly the case; though the assumption of such a right would be an infringement of the articles of union; though it may seldom or never have been avowedly claimed; yet in practice it has been constantly exercised; and would continue to be so, as long as the revenues of the confederacy should remain dependent on the intermediate agency of its members. What the consequences of the system have been, is within the knowledge of every man, the least conversant in our public affairs, and has been abundantly unfolded in different parts of these inquiries. It is this which has chiefly contributed to reduce us to a situation, that affords ample cause of mortification to ourselves, and of triumph to our enemies.

What remedy can there be for this situation, but in a change of the system which has produced it? In a change of the fallacious and delusive system of quotas and requisitions? What substitute can there be imagined for this *ignis fatuus* in finance, but that of permitting the national government to raise its own revenues by the ordinary methods of taxation, authorized in every well ordered constitution of civil government. Ingenious men may declaim with plausibility on any subject; but no human ingenuity can point out any other expedient to rescue us from the inconveniences and embarrassments, naturally resulting from defective supplies of the public treasury.

The more intelligent adversaries of the new constitution, admit the force of this reasoning; but they qualify their admission, by a distinction between what they call *internal* and *external* taxations. The former they would reserve to the state governments; the latter which they explain into commercial imposts, or rather duties on imported articles, they declare themselves willing to concede to the federal head. This distinction, however, would violate that fundamental maxim of good sense and sound policy, which dictates that every POWER ought to be proportionate to its OBJECT; and would still leave the general government in a kind of tutelage to the state governments, inconsistent with every idea of vigour or efficiency. Who can pretend that commercial imposts are, or would be, alone equal to the present and future exigencies of the union? Taking into the account the existing debt, foreign and domestic, upon any plan of extinguishment, which a man moderately impressed with the importance of public justice and public credit could approve, in addition to the establishments which all parties will acknowledge to be necessary, we could not reasonably flatter ourselves, that this resource alone, upon the most improved scale, would even suffice for its present necessities. Its future necessities admit not of calculation or limitation; and upon the principle more than once adverted to, the power of making provision for them as they arise ought to be equally unconfined. I believe it may be regarded as a position, warranted by the history of mankind, that *in the usual progress of things, the necessities of a nation, in every stage of its existence, will be found at least equal to its resources.*

To say that deficiencies may be provided for by requisitions upon the states, is on the one hand to acknowledge that this system cannot be depended upon; and on the other hand, to depend upon it for every thing beyond a certain limit. Those who have carefully attended to its vices and deformities, as they have been exhibited by experience, or delineated in the course of these papers, must feel an invincible repugnancy to trusting the national interests, in any degree to its operation. Whenever it is brought into activity, its inevitable tendency must be to enfeeble the union, and sow the seeds of discord and contention between the federal head and its members, and between the members themselves. Can it be expected that the deficiencies would be better supplied in this mode, than the total wants of the union have heretofore been supplied, in the same mode? It ought to be recollected, that if less will be required from the states, they will have proportionably less means to answer the demand. If the opinions of those who contend for the distinction which has been mentioned, were to be received as evidence of truth, one would be led to conclude, that there was some known point in the economy of national affairs, at which it would be safe to stop, and to say: thus far, the ends of public happiness will be promoted by supplying the wants of government, and all beyond this is unworthy of our care or anxiety. How is it possible that a government, half supplied and always necessitous, can fulfil the purposes of its institution; can provide for the security, advance the prosperity, or support the reputation of the commonwealth? How can it ever possess either energy or stability, dignity or credit, confidence at home, or respectability abroad? How can its administration be any thing else than a succession of expedients temporizing, impotent, disgraceful? How will it be able to avoid a frequent sacrifice of its engagements to immediate necessity? How can it undertake or execute any liberal or enlarged plans of public good?

Let us attend to what would be the effects of this situation, in the very first war in which we should happen to be engaged. We will presume, for argument sake, that the revenue arising from the import duties answers the purposes of a provision for the public debt, and of a peace establishment for the union. Thus circumstanced, a war breaks out. What would be the probable conduct of the government in such an emergency? Taught by experience, that proper dependence could not be placed on the success of requisitions; unable, by its own authority, to lay hold of fresh resources, and urged by considerations of national danger, would it not be driven to the expedient of diverting the funds already appropriated, from their proper objects to the defence of the state? It is not easy to see how a step of this kind could be avoided; and if it should be taken, it is evident that it would prove the destruction of

No. 30

public credit at the very moment that it was become essential to the public safety. To imagine that at such a crisis credit might be dispensed with, would be the extreme of infatuation. In the modern system of war, nations the most wealthy are obliged to have recourse to large loans. A country so little opulent as ours, must feel this necessity in a much stronger degree. But who would lend to a government, that prefaced its overtures for borrowing by an act which demonstrated that no reliance could be placed on the steadiness of its measures for paying? The loans it might be able to procure, would be as limited in their extent, as burthensome in their conditions. They would be made upon the same principles that usurers commonly lend to bankrupt and fraudulent debtors ... with a sparing hand, and at enormous premiums.

It may perhaps be imagined, that from the scantiness of the resources of the country, the necessity of diverting the established funds in the case supposed, would exist; though the national government should possess an unrestrained power of taxation. But two considerations will serve to quiet all apprehension on this head; one is, that we are sure the resources of the community, in their full extent, will be brought into activity for the benefit of the union; the other is, that whatever deficiencies there may be, can without difficulty be supplied by loans.

The power of creating, by its own authority, new funds from new objects of taxation, would enable the national government to borrow, as far as its necessities might require. Foreigners, as well as the citizens of America, could then reasonably repose confidence in its engagements; but to depend upon a government, that must itself depend upon thirteen other governments, for the means of fulfilling its contracts, when once its situation is clearly understood, would require a degree of credulity, not often to be met with in the pecuniary transactions of mankind, and little reconcileable with the usual sharp-sightedness of avarice.

Reflections of this kind may have trifling weight with men who hope to see the halcyon scenes of the poetic or fabulous age realized in America; but to those who believe we are likely to experience a common portion of the vicissitudes and calamities which have fallen to the lot of other nations, they must appear entitled to serious attention. Such men must behold the actual situation of their country with painful solicitude, and deprecate the evils which ambition or revenge might, with too much facility, inflict upon it.

PUBLIUS

No. 31

By Alexander Hamilton

The same subject continued

In disquisitions of every kind, there are certain primary truths, or first principles, upon which all subsequent reasonings must depend. These contain an internal evidence, which, antecedent to all reflection or combination, commands the assent of the mind. Where it produces not this effect, it must proceed either from some disorder in the organs of perception, or from the influence of some strong interest, or passion, or prejudice. Of this nature are the maxims in geometry, that the whole is greater than its part; that things equal to the same, are equal to one another; that two straight lines cannot inclose a space; and that all right angles are equal to each other. Of the same nature, are these other maxims in ethics and politics, that there cannot be an effect without a cause; that the means ought to be proportioned to the end; that every power ought to be commensurate with its object; that there ought to be no limitation of a power destined to effect a purpose which is itself incapable of limitation. And there are other truths in the two latter sciences, which, if they cannot pretend to rank in the class of axioms, are such direct inferences from them, and so obvious in themselves, and so agreeable to the natural and unsophisticated dictates of common sense, that they challenge the assent of a sound and unbiassed mind, with a degree of force and conviction almost equally irresistible.

The objects of geometrical inquiry, are so entirely abstracted from those pursuits which stir up and put in motion the unruly passions of the human heart, that mankind, without difficulty, adopt not only the more simple theorems of the science, but even those abstruse paradoxes which, however they may appear susceptible of demonstration, are at variance with the natural conceptions which the mind, without the aid of philosophy, would be led to entertain upon the subject. The INFINITE DIVISIBILITY of matter, or, in other words, the INFINITE divisibility of a FINITE thing, extending even to the minutest atom, is a point agreed among geometricians; though not less incomprehensible to common sense, than any of those mysteries in religion, against which the batteries of infidelity have been so industriously levelled.

But in the sciences of morals and politics, men are found far less tractable. To a certain degree, it is right and useful that this should be the case. Caution and investigation are a necessary armour against error and imposition. But this untractableness may be carried too far, and may degenerate into obstinancy, perverseness, or disingenuity. Though it cannot be pretended, that the principles of moral and political knowledge have, in general, the same degree of certainty with those of the mathematics; yet they have much better claims in this respect, than, to judge from the conduct of men in particular situations, we should be disposed to allow them. The obscurity is much oftener in the passions and prejudices of the reasoner, than in the subject. Men, upon too many occasions, do not give their own understandings fair play; but yielding to some untoward bias, they entangle themselves in words, and confound themselves in subtleties.

How else could it happen (if we admit the objectors to be sincere in their opposition) that positions so clear as those which manifest the necessity of a general power of taxation in the government of the union, should have to encounter any adversaries among men of discernment? Though these positions have been elsewhere fully stated, they will perhaps not be improperly recapitulated in this place, as introductory to an examination of what may have been offered by way of objection to them. They are in substance as follow:

A government ought to contain in itself every power requisite to the full accomplishment of the objects committed to its care, and to the complete execution of the trusts for which it is responsible; free from every other control but a regard to the public good and to the sense of the people.

As the duties of superintending the national defence, and of securing the public peace against foreign or domestic violence, involve a provision for casualties and dangers, to which no possible limits can be assigned, the power of making that provision ought to know no other bounds than the exigencies of the nation, and the resources of the community.

As revenue is the essential engine by which the means of answering the national exigencies must be procured, the power of procuring that article in its full extent, must necessarily be comprehended in that of providing for those exigencies.

As theory and practice conspire to prove that the power of procuring revenue is unavailing, when exercised over the states in their collective capacities, the federal government must of necessity be invested with an unqualified power of taxation in the ordinary modes.

Did not experience evince the contrary, it would be natural to conclude, that the propriety of a general power of taxation in the national government might safely be permitted to rest on the evidence of these propositions, unassisted by any additional arguments or illustrations. But we find, in fact, that the antagonists of the proposed constitution, so far from acquiescing in their justness or truth, seem to make their principal and most zealous effort against this part of the plan. It may therefore be satisfactory to analize the arguments with which they combat it.

Those of them which have been most laboured with that view, seem in substance to amount to this: "It is not true, because the exigencies of the union may not be susceptible of limitation, that its power of laying taxes ought to be unconfined. Revenue is as requisite to the purposes of the local administrations, as to those of the union; and the former are at least of equal importance with the latter, to the happiness of the people. It is therefore as necessary, that the state governments should be able to command the means of supplying their wants, as that the national government should possess the like faculty, in respect to the wants of the union. But an indefinite power of taxation in the *latter* might, and probably would, in time, deprive the *former* of the means of providing for their own necessities; and would subject them entirely to the mercy of the national legislature. As the laws of the union are to become the supreme law of the land; as it is to have power to pass all laws that may be NECESSARY for carrying into execution the authorities with which it is proposed to vestit; the national government might at any time abolish the taxes imposed for state objects, upon the pretence of an interference with its own. It might allege a necessity of doing this, in order to give efficacy to the national revenues: and thus all the resources of taxation might, by degrees, become the subjects of federal monopoly, to the entire exclusion and destruction of the state governments."

No. 31

This mode of reasoning appears sometimes to turn upon the supposition of usurpation in the national government; at other times, it seems to be designed only as a deduction from the constitutional operation of its intended powers. It is only in the latter light, that it can be admitted to have any pretensions to fairness. The moment we launch into conjectures about the usurpations of the federal government, we get into an unfathomable abyss, and fairly put ourselves out of the reach of all reasoning. Imagination may range at pleasure, till it gets bewildered amidst the labyrinths of an enchanted castle, and knows not on which side to turn to escape from the apparitions which itself has raised. Whatever may be the limits, or modifications of the powers of the union, it is easy to imagine an endless train of possible dangers; and by indulging an excess of jealousy and timidity, we may bring ourselves to a state of absolute scepticism and irresolution. I repeat here what I have observed in substance in another place, that all observations, founded upon the danger of usurpation, ought to be referred to the composition and structure of the government, not to the nature and extent of its powers. The state governments, by their original constitutions, are invested with complete sovereignty. In what does our security consist against usurpations from that quarter? Doubtless in the manner of their formation, and in a due dependence of those who are to administer them upon the people. If the proposed construction of the federal government be found, upon an impartial examination of it, to be such as to afford, to a proper extent, the same species of security, all apprehensions on the score of usurpation ought to be discarded.

It should not be forgotten, that a disposition in the state governments to encroach upon the rights of the union, is quite as probable as a disposition in the union to encroach upon the rights of the state governments. What side would be likely to prevail in such a conflict, must depend on the means which the contending parties could employ, towards insuring success. As in republics, strength is always on the side of the people; and as there are weighty reasons to induce a belief, that the state governments will commonly possess most influence over them, the natural conclusion is, that such contests will be most apt to end to the disadvantage of the union; and that there is greater probability of encroachments by the members upon the federal head, than by the federal head upon the members. But it is evident, that all conjectures of this kind must be extremely vague and fallible; and that it is by far the safest course to lay them altogether aside; and to confine our attention wholly to the nature and extent of the powers, as they are delineated in the constitution. Every thing beyond this, must be left to the prudence and firmness of the people; who, as they will hold the scales in their own hands, it is to be hoped, will always take care to preserve the constitutional equilibrium between the general and the state governments. Upon this ground, which is evidently the true one, it will not be difficult to obviate the objections, which have been made to an indefinite power of taxation in the United States.

PUBLIUS

No. 32

by Alexander Hamilton

The same subject continued

Although I am of opinion that there would be no real danger of the consequences to the state governments, which seem to be apprehended from a power in the union to control them in the levies of money; because I am persuaded that the sense of the people, the extreme hazard of provoking the resentments of the state governments, and a conviction of the utility and necessity of local administrations, for local purposes, would be a complete barrier against the oppressive use of such a power: yet I am willing here to allow, in its full extent, the justness of the reasoning, which requires, that the individual states should possess an independent and uncontrolable authority to raise their own revenues for the supply of their own wants. And making this concession, I affirm, that (with the sole exception of duties on imports and exports) they would, under the plan of the convention, retain that authority in the most absolute and unqualified sense; and that an attempt on the part of the national government to abridge them in the exercise of it, would be a violent assumption of power, unwarranted by any article or clause of its constitution.

An entire consolidation of the states into one complete national sovereignty, would imply an entire subordination of the parts; and whatever powers might remain in them, would be altogether dependent on the general will. But as the plan of the convention aims only at a partial union or consolidation, the state governments would clearly retain all the rights of sovereignty which they before had, and which were not, by that act, *exclusively* delegated to the United States. This exclusive delegation, or rather this alienation of state sovereignty, would only exist in three cases: where the constitution in express terms granted an exclusive authority to the union; where it granted, in one instance, an authority to the union, and in another, prohibited the states from exercising the like authority; and where it granted an authority to the union, to which a similar authority in the states would be absolutely and totally *contradictory* and *repugnant*. I use these terms to distinguish this last case from another which might appear to resemble it; but which would, in fact, be essentially different: I mean where the exercise of a concurrent jurisdiction, might be productive of occasional interferences in the *policy* of any branch of administration, but would not imply any direct contradiction or repugnancy in point of constitutional authority. These three cases of exclusive jurisdiction in the federal government, may be exemplified by the following instances: the last clause but one in the eighth section of the first article, provides expressly, that congress shall exercise "*exclusive legislation*" over the district to be appropriated as the seat of government. This answers to the first case. The first clause of the same section impowers congress "*to lay and collect taxes, duties, imposts, and excises;*" and the second clause of the tenth section of the same article declares, that "*no state shall,* without the consent of congress, *lay any imposts or duties on imports or exports,* except for the purpose of executing its inspection laws." Hence would result an exclusive power in the union to lay duties on imports and exports, with the particular exception mentioned; but this power is abridged by another clause, which declares, that no tax or duty shall be laid on articles exported from any state; in consequence of which qualification, it now only extends to the *duties on imports*. This answers to the second case. The third will be found in that clause which declares, that congress shall have power "to establish an UNIFORM RULE of naturalization throughout the United States." This must necessarily be exclusive; because if each state had power to prescribe a DISTINCT RULE, there could be no UNIFORM RULE.

A case which may perhaps be thought to resemble the latter, but which is in fact widely different affects the question immediately under consideration. I mean the power of imposing taxes on all articles other than exports and imports. This, I contend, is manifestly a concurrent and co-equal authority in the United States and in the individual states. There is plainly no expression in the granting clause, which makes that power *exclusive* in the union. There is no independent clause or sentence which prohibits the states from exercising it. So far is this from being the case, that a plain and conclusive argument to the contrary is deducible, from the restraint laid upon the states in relation to duties on imports and exports. This restriction implies an admission, that if it were not inserted, the states would possess the power it excludes; and it implies a further admission, that as to all other taxes, the authority of the states remains undiminished. In any other view it would be both unnecessary and dangerous. It would be unnecessary, because if the grant to the union of the power of laying such duties, implied the exclusion of the states, or even their subordination in this particular, there could be no need of such a restriction: it would be dangerous, because the introduction of it leads directly to the conclusion which has been mentioned, and which, if the reasoning of the objectors be just, could not have been intended; I mean that the states, in all cases to which the restriction did not apply, would have a concurrent power of taxation with the union. The restriction in question amounts to what lawyers call a NEGATIVE PREGNANT; that is, a *negation* of one thing, and an *affirmance* of another; a negation of the authority of the states to impose taxes on imports and exports, and an affirmance of their authority to impose them on all other articles. It would be mere sophistry to argue that it was meant to exclude them *absolutely* from the imposition of taxes of the former kind, and to leave them at liberty to lay others *subject to the control* of the national legislature. The restraining or prohibitory clause only says, that they shall not, *without the consent of congress,* lay such duties; and if we are to understand this in the sense last mentioned, the constitution would then be made to introduce a formal provision, for the sake of a very absurd conclusion; which is, that the states, *with the consent* of the national legislature, might tax imports and exports; and that they might tax every other article, *unless controled* by the same body. If this was the intention, why was it not left, in the first instance, to what is alleged to be the natural operation of the original clause, conferring a general power of taxation upon the union? It is evident that this could not have been the intention, and that it will not bear a construction of the kind.

No. 32

As to a supposition of repugnancy between the power of taxation in the states and in the union, it cannot be supported in that sense which would be requisite to work an exclusion of the states. It is indeed possible that a tax might be laid on a particular article by a state, which might render it *inexpedient* that a further tax should be laid on the same article by the union; but it would not imply a constitutional inability to impose a further tax. The quantity of the imposition, the expediency or inexpediency of an increase on either side, would be mutually questions of prudence; but there would be involved no direct contradiction of power. The particular policy of the national and of the state system of finance might now and then not exactly coincide, and might require reciprocal forbearances. It is not however a mere possibility of inconvenience in the exercise of powers, but an immediate constitutional repugnancy, that can by implication alienate and extinguish a pre-existing right of sovereignty.

The necessity of a concurrent jurisdiction in certain cases, results from the division of the sovereign power; and the rule that all authorities, of which the states are not explicitly divested in favour of the union, remain with them in full vigour, is not only a theoretical consequence of that division, but is clearly admitted by the whole tenor of the instrument which contains the articles of the proposed constitution. We there find, that notwithstanding the affirmative grants of general authorities, there has been the most pointed care in those cases where it was deemed improper that the like authorities should reside in the states, to insert negative clauses prohibiting the exercise of them by the states. The tenth section of the first article consists altogether of such provisions. This circumstance is a clear indication of the sense of the convention, and furnishes a rule of interpretation out of the body of the act, which justifies the position I have advanced, and refutes every hypothesis to the contrary.

PUBLIUS

No. 33

by Alexander Hamilton

The same subject continued

The residue of the argument against the provisions of the constitution, in respect to taxation, is ingrafted upon the following clauses: The last clause of the eighth section of the first article, authorizes the national legislature "to make all laws which shall be *necessary* and *proper,* for carrying into execution *the powers* by that constitution vested in the government of the United States, or in any department or officer thereof;" and the second clause of the sixth article declares, that "the constitution and the laws of the United States made *in pursuance thereof,* and the treaties made by their authority, shall be the *supreme law* of the land; any thing in the constitution or laws of any state to the contrary notwithstanding."

These two clauses have been the sources of much virulent invective, and petulant declamation, against the proposed constitution. They have been held up to the people in all the exaggerated colours of misrepresentation; as the pernicious engines by which their local governments were to be destroyed, and their liberties exterminated; as the hideous monster whose devouring jaws would spare neither sex nor age, nor high nor low, nor sacred nor profane; and yet, strange as it may appear, after all this clamour, to those who may not have happened to contemplate them in the same light, it may be affirmed with perfect confidence, that the constitutional operation of the intended government would be precisely the same, if these clauses were entirely obliterated, as if they were repeated in every article. They are only declaratory of a truth, which would have resulted by necessary and unavoidable implication from the very act of constituting a federal government, and vesting it with certain specified powers. This is so clear a proposition, that moderation itself can scarcely listen to the railings which have been so copiously vented against this part of the plan, without emotions that disturb its equanimity.

What is a power, but the ability or faculty of doing a thing? What is the ability to do a thing, but the power of employing the *means* necessary to its execution? What is a LEGISLATIVE power, but a power of making LAWS? What are the *means* to execute a LEGISLATIVE power, but LAWS? What is the power of laying and collecting taxes, but a *legislative power,* or a power of *making laws,* to lay and collect taxes? What are the proper means of executing such a power, but *necessary* and *proper* laws?

This simple train of inquiry furnishes us at once with a test of the true nature of the clause complained of. It conducts us to this palpable truth, that a power to lay and collect taxes, must be a power to pass all laws *necessary* and *proper* for the execution of that power: and what does the unfortunate and calumniated provision in question do, more than declare the same truth; to wit, that the national legislature to whom the power of laying and collecting taxes had been previously given, might, in the execution of that power, pass all laws *necessary* and *proper* to carry it into effect? I have applied these observations thus particularly to the power of taxation; because it is the immediate subject under consideration, and because it is the most important of the authorities proposed to be conferred upon the union. But the same process will lead to the same result, in relation to all other powers declared in the constitution. And it is *expressly* to execute these powers, that the sweeping clause, as it has been affectedly called, authorizes the national legislature to pass all *necessary* and *proper* laws. If there be any thing exceptionable, it must be sought for in the specific powers, upon which this general declaration is predicated. The declaration itself, though it may be chargeable with tautology or redundancy, is at least perfectly harmless.

But SUSPICION may ask, why then was it introduced? The answer is, that it could only have been done for greater caution, and to guard against all cavilling refinements in those who might hereafter feel a disposition to curtail and evade the legitimate authorities of the union. The convention probably foresaw, what it has been a principal aim of these papers to inculcate, that the danger which most threatens our political welfare, is, that the state governments will finally sap the foundations of the union; and might therefore think it necessary, in so cardinal a point, to leave nothing to construction. Whatever may have been the inducement to it, the wisdom of the precaution is evident from the cry which has been raised against it; as that very cry betrays a disposition to question the great and essential truth which it is manifestly the object of that provision to declare.

But it may be again asked, who is to judge of the *necessity* and *propriety* of the laws to be passed for executing the powers of the union? I answer, first, that this question arises as well and as fully upon the simple grant of those powers, as upon the declaratory clause: and I answer, in the second place, that the national government, like every other, must judge, in the first instance, of the proper exercise of its powers; and its constituents in the last. If the federal government should overpass the just bounds of its authority, and make a tyrannical use of its powers; the people, whose creature it is, must appeal to the standard they have formed, and take such measures to redress the injury done to the constitution, as the exigency may suggest and prudence justify. The propriety of a law, in a constitutional light, must always be determined by the nature of the powers upon which it is founded. Suppose, by some forced construction of its authority (which indeed cannot easily be imagined) the federal legislature should attempt to vary the law of descent in any state; would it not be evident, that in making such an attempt, it had exceeded its jurisdiction, and infringed upon that of the state? Suppose, again, that upon the pretence of an interference with its revenues, it should undertake to abrogate a land tax imposed by the authority of a state; would it not be equally evident, that this was an invasion of that concurrent jurisdiction in respect to this species of tax, which the constitution plainly supposes to exist in the state governments? If there ever should be a doubt on this head, the credit of it will be entirely due to those reasoners, who, in the imprudent zeal of their animosity to the plan of the convention, have laboured to envelope it in a cloud, calculated to obscure the plainest and simplest truths.

But it is said, that the laws of the union are to be the *supreme law* of the land. What inference can be drawn from this, or what would they amount to, if they were not to be supreme? It is evident they would amount to nothing. A LAW, by the very meaning of the term, includes supremacy. It is a rule, which those to whom it is prescribed are bound to observe. This results from every political association. If individuals enter into a state of society, the laws of that society must be the supreme regulator of their conduct. If a number of political societies enter into a larger political society, the laws which the latter may enact, pursuant to the powers intrusted to it by its constitution, must necessarily be supreme over those societies, and the individuals of whom they are composed. It would otherwise be a mere treaty, dependent on the good faith of the parties, and not a government; which is only another word for POLITICAL POWER AND SUPREMACY. But it will not follow from this doctrine, that acts of the larger society, which are *not pursuant* to its constitutional powers, but which are invasions of the residuary authorities of the smaller societies, will become the supreme law of the land. These will be merely acts of usurpation, and will deserve to be treated as such. Hence we perceive, that the clause which declares the supremacy of the laws of the union, like the one we have just before considered, only declares a truth, which flows immediately and necessarily from the institution of a federal government. It will not, I presume, have escaped observation, that it *expressly* confines this supremacy to laws made *pursuant to the constitution;* which I mention merely as an instance of caution in the convention; since that limitation would have been to be understood, though it had not been expressed.

Though a law, therefore, laying a tax for the use of the United States would be supreme in its nature, and could not legally be opposed or controled; yet, a law abrogating or preventing the collection of a tax laid by the authority of a state, (unless upon imports and exports) would not be the supreme law of the land, but an usurpation of a power not granted by the constitution. As far as an improper accumulation of taxes, on the same object, might tend to render the collection difficult or precarious, this would be a mutual inconvenience, not arising from a superiority or defect of power on either side, but from an injudicious exercise of power by one or the other, in a manner equally disadvantageous to both. It is to be hoped and presumed, however, that mutual interests would dictate a concert in this respect, which would avoid any material inconvenience. The inference from the whole is . . . that the individual states would, under the proposed constitution, retain an independent and uncontrolable authority to raise revenue to any extent of which they may stand in need, by every kind of taxation, except duties on imports and exports. It will be shown in the next paper, that this *concurrent jurisdiction* in the article of taxation, was the only admissible substitute for an entire subordination, in respect to this branch of power, of state authority to that of the union.

PUBLIUS

No. 34

by Alexander Hamilton

The same subject continued

I flatter myself it has been clearly shown in my last number, that the particular states, under the proposed constitution, would have CO-EQUAL authority with the union in the article of revenue, except as to duties on imports. As this leaves open to the states far the greatest part of the resources of the community, there can be no colour for the assertion, that they would not possess means as abundant as could be desired, for the supply of their own wants, independent of all external control. That the field is sufficiently wide, will more fully appear, when we come to develope the inconsiderable share of the public expenses, for which it will fall to the lot of the state governments to provide.

To argue upon abstract principles, that this co-ordinate authority cannot exist, would be to set up theory and supposition against fact and reality. However proper such reasonings might be, to show that a thing *ought not to exist*, they are wholly to be rejected, when they are made use of to prove that it does not exist, contrary to the evidence of the fact itself. It is well known, that in the Roman republic, the legislative authority in the last resort, resided for ages in two different political bodies . . . not as branches of the same legislature, but as distinct and independent legislatures; in each of which an opposite interest prevailed: in one, the Patrician; in the other the Plebeian. Many arguments might have been adduced, to prove the unfitness of two such seemingly contradictory authorities, each having power to *annul* or *repeal* the acts of the other. But a man would have been regarded as frantic, who should have attempted at Rome to disprove their existence. It will readily be understood, that I allude to the COMITIA CENTURIATA and the COMITIA TRIBUTIA. The former, in which the people voted by centuries, was so arranged as to give a superiority to the Patrician interest. In the latter, in

No. 34

which numbers prevailed, the Plebeian interest had an entire predominancy. And yet these two legislatures co-existed for ages, and the Roman republic attained to the pinnacle of human greatness.

In the case particularly under consideration, there is no such contradiction as appears in the example cited: there is no power on either side to annul the acts of the other. And in practice, there is little reason to apprehend any inconvenience; because, in a short course of time, the wants of the states will naturally reduce themselves within *a very narrow compass:* and in the interim, the United States will, in all probability, find it convenient to abstain wholly from those objects to which the particular states would be inclined to resort.

To form a more precise judgment of the true merits of this question, it will be well to advert to the proportion between the objects that will require a federal provision in respect to revenue, and those which will require a state provision. We shall discover that the former are altogether unlimited: and that the latter are circumscribed within very moderate bounds. In pursuing this inquiry, we must bear in mind, that we are not to confine our view to the present period, but to look forward to remote futurity. Constitutions of civil government are not to be framed upon a calculation of existing exigencies; but upon a combination of these, with the probable exigencies of ages, according to the natural and tried course of human affairs. Nothing, therefore, can be more fallacious, than to infer the extent of any power proper to be lodged in the national government, from an estimate of its immediate necessities. There ought to be a CAPACITY to provide for future contingencies, as they may happen; and as these are illimitable in their nature, so it is impossible safely to limit that capacity. It is true, perhaps, that a computation might be made, with sufficient accuracy to answer the purpose, of the quantity of revenue requisite to discharge the subsisting engagements of the union, and to maintain those establishments which, for some time to come, would suffice in time of peace. But would it be wise, or would it not rather be the extreme of folly, to stop at this point, and to leave the government intrusted with the care of the national defence, in a state of absolute incapacity to provide for the protection of the community, against future invasions of the public peace, by foreign war or domestic convulsions? If we must be obliged to exceed this point, where can we stop short of an indefinite power of providing for emergencies as they may arise? Though it be easy to assert, in general terms, the possibility of forming a rational judgment of a due provision against probable dangers; yet we may safely challenge those who make the assertion, to bring forward their data, and may affirm, that they would be found as vague and uncertain as any that could be produced to establish the probable duration of the world. Observations, confined to the mere prospects of internal attacks, can deserve no weight; though even these will admit of no satisfactory calculations: but if we mean to be a commercial people, it must form a part of our policy to be able one day to defend that commerce. The support of a navy, and of naval wars, would involve contingencies that must baffle all the efforts of political arithmetic.

Admitting that we ought to try the novel and absurd experiment in politics, of tying up the hands of government from offensive war, founded upon reasons of state: yet, certainly, we ought not to disable it from guarding the community against the ambition or enmity of other nations. A cloud has been for some time hanging over the European world. If it should break forth into a storm, who can insure us, that in its progress a part of its fury would not be spent upon us? No reasonable man would hastily pronounce that we are entirely out of its reach. Or if the combustible materials that now seem to be collecting, should be dissipated without coming to maturity; or if a flame should be kindled without extending to us; what security can we have that our tranquillity will long remain undisturbed from some other cause, or from some other quarter? Let us recollect, that peace or war will not always be left to our option; that however moderate or unambitious we may be, we cannot count upon the moderation, or hope to extinguish the ambition, of others. Who could have imagined, at the conclusion of the last war, that France and Britain, wearied and exhausted as they both were, would already have looked with so hostile an aspect upon each other? To judge from the history of mankind, we shall be compelled to conclude, that the fiery and destructive passions of war reign in the human breast with much more powerful sway, than the mild and beneficent sentiments of peace; and that to model our political systems upon speculations of lasting tranquillity, would be to calculate on the weaker springs of the human character.

What are the chief sources of expense in every government? What has occasioned that enormous accumulation of debts with which several of the European nations are oppressed? The answer plainly is, wars and rebellious; the support of those institutions which are necessary to guard the body politic against these two most mortal diseases of society. The expenses arising from those institutions which relate to the mere domestic police of a state, to the support of its legislative, executive, and judiciary departments, with their different appendages, and to the encouragement of agriculture and manufactures, (which will comprehend almost all the objects of state expenditure) are insignificant in comparison with those which relate to the national defence.

In the kingdom of Great Britain, where all the ostentatious apparatus of monarchy is to be provided for, not above a fifteenth part of the annual income of the nation is appropriated to the class of expenses last mentioned: the other fourteen fifteenths are absorbed in the payment of the interest of debts contracted for carrying on the wars in which that country has been engaged, and in the maintenance of fleets and armies. If, on the one hand, it should be observed, that the expenses incurred in the prosecution of the ambitions enterprises and vain glorious pursuits of a monarchy, are not a proper standard by which to judge of those which might be necessary in a republic; it ought, on the other hand, to be remarked, that there should be as great a disproportion between the profusion and extravagance of a wealthy kingdom in its domestic administration, and the frugality and economy which, in that particular, become the modest simplicity of republican government. If we balance a proper deduction from one side, against that which it is supposed ought to be made from the other, the proportion may still be considered as holding good.

But let us take a view of the large debt which we have ourselves contracted in a single war, and let us only calculate on a common share of the events which disturb the peace of nations, and we shall instantly perceive, without the aid of any elaborate illustration, that there must always be an immense disproportion between the objects of federal and state expenditure. It is true, that several of the states, separately, are incumbered with considerable debts, which are an excresence of the late war. But this cannot happen again, if the proposed system be adopted; and when these debts are discharged, the only call for revenue of any consequence, which the state governments will continue to experience, will be for the mere support of their respective civil lists; to which, if we add all contingencies, the total amount in every state ought to fall considerably short of a million of dollars.

If it cannot be denied to be a just principle, that in framing a constitution of government for a nation, we ought, in those provisions which are designed to be permanent, to calculate, not on temporary, but on permanent causes of expense; our attention would be directed to a provision in favour of the state governments for an annual sum of about 1,000,000 dollars; while the exigencies of the union could be susceptible of no limits, even in imagination. In this view of the subject, by what logic can it be maintained, that the local governments ought to command, in perpetuity, an *exclusive* source of revenue for any sum beyond that which has been stated? To extend its power further, in *exclusion* of the authority of the union, would be to take the resources of the community out of those hands which stood in need of them for the public welfare, in order to put them into other hands which could have no just or proper occasion for them.

Suppose then, the convention had been inclined to proceed upon the principle of a repartition of the objects of revenue, between the union and its members in *proportion* to their comparative necessities; what particular fund could have been selected for the use of the states, that would not either have been too much or too little; too little for their present, too much for their future wants. As to the line of separation between external and internal taxes, this would leave to the states, at a rough computation, the command of two-thirds of the resources of the community to defray from a tenth to a twentieth of its expenses; and to the union, one third of the resources of the community to defray from nine-tenths to nineteen twentieths of its expenses. If we desert this boundary, and content ourselves with leaving to the states an exclusive power of taxing houses and lands, there would still be a great disproportion between the *means* and the *end;* the possession of one-third of the resources of the community to supply, at most, one-tenth of its wants. If any fund could have been selected, and appropriated, equal to and not greater than the object, it would have been inadequate to the discharge of the existing debts of the particular states, and would have left them dependent on the union for a provision for this purpose.

The preceding train of observations will justify the position which has been elsewhere laid down, that "A CONCURRENT JURISDICTION in the article of taxation, was the only admissible substitute for an entire subordination, in respect to this branch of power, of state authority to that of the union." Any separation of the objects of revenue that could have been fallen upon, would have amounted to a sacrifice of the great INTERESTS of the union to the POWER of the individual states. The convention thought the concurrent jurisdiction preferable to that subordination; and it is evident that it has at least the merit of reconciling an indefinite constitutional power of taxation in the federal government, with an adequate and independent power in the states to provide for their own necessities. There remain a few other lights, in which this important subject of taxation will claim a further consideration.

PUBLIUS

No. 35

by Alexander Hamilton

The same subject continued

Before we proceed to examine any other objections to an indefinite power of taxation in the union, I shall make one general remark; which is, that if the jurisdiction of the national government, in the article of revenue, should be restricted to particular objects, it would naturally occasion an undue proportion of the public burthens to fall upon those objects. Two evils would spring from this source ... the oppression of particular branches of industry, and an unequal distribution of the taxes, as well among the several states, as among the citizens of the same state.

Suppose, as has been contended for, the federal power of taxation were to be confined to duties on imports; it is evident that the government, for want of being able to command other resources, would frequently be tempted to extend these duties to an injurious excess. There are persons who imagine that this can never be the case; since the higher they are, the more it is alleged they will tend to discourage an extravagant consumption, to produce a favourable balance of trade, and to promote domestic manufactures. But all extremes are pernicious in various ways. Exorbitant duties on imported articles serve to beget a general spirit of smuggling; which is always prejudicial to the fair trader, and eventually to the revenue itself: they tend to render other classes of the community tributary, in an improper degree, to the manufacturing classes, to whom they give a premature monopoly of the markets: they sometimes force industry out of its most natural channels into others in which it flows with less advantage: and in the last place, they oppress the merchant, who is often obliged to pay them himself without any retribution from the consumer. When the demand is equal to the quantity of goods at market, the consumer generally pays the duty; but when the markets happen to be overstocked, a great proportion falls upon the merchant, and sometimes not only exhausts his profits but breaks in upon his capital. I am apt to think, that a division of the duty, between the seller and the buyer, more often happens than is commonly imagined. It is not always possible to raise the price of a commodity, in exact proportion to every additional imposition laid upon it. The merchant, especially in a country of small commercial capital, is often under a necessity of keeping prices down in order to a more expeditious sale.

The maxim, that the consumer is the payer, is so much oftener true than the reverse of the proposition, that it is far more equitable that the duties on imports should go into a common stock, than that they should redound to the exclusive benefit of the importing states. But it is not so generally true, as to render it equitable, that those duties should form the only national fund. When they are paid by the merchant, they operate as an additional tax upon the importing state; whose citizens pay their proportion of them in the character of consumers. In this view, they are productive of inequality among the states; which inequality would be increased with the increased extent of the duties. The confinement of the national revenues to this species of imposts, would be attended with inequality, from a different cause, between the manufacturing and the non-manufacturing states. The states which can go furthest towards the supply of their own wants, by their own manufactures, will not, according to their numbers or wealth, consume so great a proportion of imported articles, as those states which are not in the same favourable situation. They would not, therefore, in this mode alone, contribute to the public treasury in a ratio to their abilities. To make them do this, it is necessary that recourse be had to excises; the proper objects of which are particular kinds of manufactures. New York is more deeply interested in these considerations, than such of her citizens as contend for limiting the power of the union to external taxation, may be aware of. New York is an importing state, and from a greater disproportion between her population and territory, is less likely, than some other states, speedily to become in any considerable degree a manufacturing state. She would of course suffer, in a double light, from restraining the jurisdiction of the union to commercial imposts.

So far as these observations tend to inculcate a danger of the import duties being extended to an injurious extreme, it may be observed, conformably to a remark made in another part of these papers, that the interest of the revenue itself would be a sufficient guard against such an extreme. I readily admit that this would be the case, as long as other resources were open; but if the avenues to them were closed, HOPE, stimulated by necessity, might beget experiments, fortified by rigorous precautions and additional penalties; which, for a time, might have the intended effect, till there had been leisure to contrive expedients to elude these new precautions. The first success would be apt to inspire false opinions; which it might require a long course of subsequent experience to correct. Necessity, especially in politics, often occasions false hopes, false reasonings, and a system of measures correspondently erroneous. But even if this supposed excess should not be a consequence of the limitation of the federal power of taxation, the inequalities spoken of would still ensue, though not in the same degree, from the other causes that have been noticed. Let us now return to the examination of objections.

One which, if we may judge from the frequency of its repetition, seems most to be relied on, is, that the house of representatives is not sufficiently numerous for the reception of all the different classes of citizens; in order to combine the interests and feelings of every part of the community, and to produce a due sympathy between the representative body and its constituents. This argument presents itself under a very specious and seducing form; and is well calculated to lay hold of the prejudices of those to whom it is addressed. But when we come to dissect it with attention, it will appear to be made up of nothing but fair sounding words. The object it seems to aim at, is in the first place impracticable, and in the sense in which it is contended for is unnecessary. I reserve for another place, the discussion of the question which relates to the sufficiency of the representative body in respect to numbers; and shall content myself with examining here the particular use which has been made of a contrary supposition, in reference to the immediate subject of our inquiries.

The idea of an actual representation of all classes of the people, by persons of each class, is altogether visionary. Unless it were expressly provided in the constitution, that each different occupation should send one or more members, the thing would never take place in practice. Mechanics and manufacturers will always be inclined, with few exceptions, to give their votes to merchants, in preference to persons of their own professions or trades. Those discerning citizens are well aware, that the mechanic and manufacturing arts furnish the materials of mercantile enterprise and industry. Many of them, indeed, are immediately connected with the operations of commerce. They know that the merchant is their natural patron and friend; and they are aware, that however great the confidence they may justly feel in their own good sense, their interests can be more effectually promoted by the merchant than by themselves. They are sensible that their habits of life have not been such as to give them those acquired endowments, without which, in a deliberative assembly, the greatest natural abilities are for the most part useless; and that the influence and weight, and superior acquirements of the merchants, render them more equal to a contest with any spirit which might happen to infuse itself into the public councils, unfriendly to the manufacturing and trading interests. These considerations, and many others that might be mentioned, prove, and experience confirms it, that artizans and manufacturers will commonly be disposed to bestow their votes upon merchants and those whom they recommend. We must therefore consider merchants as the natural representatives of all these classes of the community.

With regard to the learned professions, little need be observed: they truly form no distinct interest in society; and according to their situation and talents, will be indiscriminately the objects of the confidence and choice of each other, and of other parts of the community.

Nothing remains but the landed interest; and this, in a political view, and particularly in relation to taxes, I take to be perfectly united, from the wealthiest landlord, down to the poorest tenant. No tax can be laid on land which will not affect the proprietor of thousands of acres, as well as the proprietor of a single acre. Every landholder will therefore have a common interest to keep the taxes on land as low as possible; and common interest may always be reckoned upon as the surest bond of sympathy. But if we even could suppose a distinction of interests between the opulent landholder, and the middling farmer, what reason is there to conclude, that the first would stand a better chance of being deputed to the national legislature than the last? If we take fact as our guide, and look into our own senate and assembly, we shall find that moderate proprietors of land prevail in both; nor is this less the case in the senate, which consists of a smaller number, than in the assembly, which is composed of a greater number. Where the qualifications of the electors are the same, whether they have to choose a small or a large number, their votes will fall upon those in whom they have most confidence; whether these happen to be men of large fortunes or of moderate property, or of no property at all.

It is said to be necessary that all classes of citizens should have some of their own number in the representative body, in order that their feelings and interests may be the better understood and attended to. But we have seen that this will never happen under any arrangement that leaves the votes of the people free. Where this is the case, the representative body, with too few exceptions to have any influence on the spirit of the government, will be composed of landholders, merchants, and men of the learned professions. But where is the danger that the interests and feelings of the different classes of citizens will not be understood or attended to by these three descriptions of men? Will not the landholder know and feel whatever will promote or injure the interests of landed property? and will he not, from his own interest in that species of property, be sufficiently prone to resist every attempt to prejudice or encumber it? Will not the merchant understand and be disposed to cultivate, as far as may be proper, the interests of the mechanic and manufacturing arts, to which his commerce is so nearly allied? Will not the man of the learned profession, who will feel a neutrality to the rivalships among the different branches of industry, be likely to prove an impartial arbiter between them, ready to promote either, so far as it shall appear to him conducive to the general interests of the community?

If we take into the account the momentary humours or dispositions which may happen to prevail in particular parts of the society, and to which a wise administration will never be inattentive, is the man whose situation leads to extensive inquiry and information less likely to be a competent judge of their nature, extent, and foundation, than one whose observation does not travel beyond the circle of his neighbours and acquaintances? Is it not natural that a man who is a candidate for the favour of the people, and who is dependent on the suffrages of his fellow citizens for the continuance of his public honours, should take care to inform himself of their dispositions and inclinations, and should be willing to allow them their proper degree of influence upon his conduct? This dependence, and the necessity of being bound himself, and his posterity, by the laws to which he gives his assent, are the true, and they are the strong chords of sympathy between the representative and the constituent.

There is no part of the administration of government that requires extensive information, and a thorough knowledge of the principles of political economy, so much as the business of taxation. The man who understands those principles best, will be least likely to resort to oppressive expedients, or to sacrifice any particular class of citizens to the procurement of revenue. It might be demonstrated that the most productive system of finance will always be the least burthensome. There can be no doubt that, in order to a judicious exercise of the power of taxation, it is necessary that the person in whose hands it is, should be acquainted with the general genius, habits, and modes of thinking of the people at large, and with the resources of the country. And this is all that can be reasonably meant by a knowledge of the interests and feelings of the people. In any other sense, the proposition has either no meaning, or an absurd one. And in that sense, let every considerate citizen judge for himself, where the requisite qualification is most likely to be found.

PUBLIUS

No. 36

by Alexander Hamilton

The same subject continued

We have seen that the result of the observations to which the foregoing number has been principally devoted, is, that from the natural operation of the different interests and views of the various classes of the community, whether the representation of the people be more or less numerous, it will consist almost entirely of proprietors of land, of merchants, and of members of the learned professions, who will truly represent all those different interests and views. If it should be objected, that we have seen other descriptions of men in the local legislatures; I answer, that it is admitted there are exceptions to the rule, but not in sufficient number to influence the general complexion or character of the government. There are strong minds in every walk of life, that will rise superior to the disadvantages of situation, and will command the tribute due to their merit, not only from the classes to which they particularly belong, but from the society in general. The door ought to be equally open to all; and I trust, for the credit of human nature, that we shall see examples of such vigorous plants flourishing in the soil of federal, as well as of state legislation; but occasional instances of this sort, will not render the reasoning, founded upon the general course of things, less conclusive.

The subject might be placed in several other lights, that would all lead to the same result; and in particular it might be asked, what greater affinity or relation of interest can be conceived between the carpenter and blacksmith, and the linen manufacturer or stocking weaver, than between the merchant and either of them? It is notorious, that there are often as great rivalships between different branches of the mechanic or manufacturing arts, as there are between any of the departments of labour and industry; so that unless the representative body were to be far more numerous, than would be consistent with any idea of regularity or wisdom in its deliberation, it is impossible that what seems to be the spirit of the objection we have been considering, should ever be realized in practice. But I forbear to dwell longer on a matter, which has hitherto worn too loose a garb to admit even of an accurate inspection of its real shape or tendency.

There is another objection of a somewhat more precise nature, which claims our attention. It has been asserted that a power of internal taxation in the national legislature, could never be exercised with advantage, as well from the want of a sufficient knowledge of local circumstances, as from an interference between the revenue laws of the union, and of the particular states. The supposition of a want of proper knowledge, seems to be entirely destitute of foundation. If any question is depending in a state legislature, respecting one of the counties, which demands a knowledge of local details, how is it acquired? No doubt from the information of the members of the county. Cannot the like knowledge be obtained in the national legislature, from the representatives of each state? And is it not to be presumed, that the men who will generally be sent there, will be possessed of the necessary degree of intelligence, to be able to communicate that information? Is the knowledge of local circumstances, as applied to taxation, a minute topographical acquaintance with all the mountains, rivers, streams, highways, and bye-paths in each state? Or is it a general acquaintance with its situation, and resources . . . with the state of its agriculture, commerce, manufactures . . . with the nature of its products and consumptions . . . with the different degrees and kinds of its wealth, property and industry?

Nations in general, even under governments of the more popular kind, usually commit the administration of their finances to single men, or to boards composed of a few individuals, who digest and prepare, in the first instance, the plans of taxation; which are afterwards passed into law by the authority of the sovereign or legislature. Inquisitive and enlightened statesmen, are every where deemed best qualified to make a judicious selection of the objects proper for revenue; which is a clear indication, as far as the sense of mankind can have weight in the question, of the species of knowledge of local circumstances, requisite to the purposes of taxation.

The taxes intended to be comprised under the general denomination of internal taxes, may be sub-divided into those of the *direct,* and those of the *indirect* kind. Though the objection be made to both, yet the reasoning upon it seems to be confined to the former branch. And indeed as to the latter, by which must be understood duties and excises on articles of consumption, one is at a loss to conceive, what can be the nature of the difficulties apprehended. The knowledge relating to them, must evidently be of a kind, that will either be suggested by the nature of the article itself, or can easily be procured from any well informed man, especially of the mercantile class. The circumstances that may distinguish its situation in one state, from its situation in another, must be few, simple, and easy to be comprehended. The principal thing to be attended to, would be to avoid those articles which had been previously appropriated to the use of a particular state; and there could be no difficulty in ascertaining the revenue system of each. This could always be known from the respective codes of laws, as well as from the information of the members of the several states.

The objection, when applied to real property, or to houses and lands, appears to have, at first sight, more foundation; but even in this view, it will not bear a close examination. Land taxes are commonly laid in one of two modes, either by *actual* valuations, permanent or periodical, or by occasional assessments, at the discretion, or according to the best judgment of certain officers, whose duty it is to make them. In either case, the EXECUTION of the business, which alone requires the knowledge of local details, must be confided to discreet persons in the character of commissioners or assessors, elected by the people, or appointed by the government for the purpose. All that the law can do, must be to name the persons, or to prescribe the manner of their election or appointment; to fix their numbers and qualifications, and to draw the general outlines of ther powers and duties. And what is there in all this, that cannot as well be performed by the national legislature, as by the state legislature? The attention of either, can only reach to general principles: local details, as already observed, must be referred to those who are to execute the plan.

But there is a simple point of view, in which this matter may be placed, that must be altogether satisfactory. The national legislature can make use of the *system of each state within that state*. The method of laying and collecting this species of taxes in each state, can, in all its parts, be adopted and employed by the federal government.

Let it be recollected, that the proportion of these taxes is not to be left to the discretion of the national legislature: but it is to be determined by the numbers of each state, as described in the second section of the first article. An actual census, or enumeration of the people, must furnish the rule; a circumstance which effectually shuts the door to partiality or oppression. The abuse of this power of taxation seems to have been provided against with guarded circumspection. In addition to the precaution just mentioned, there is a provision that "all duties imposts and excises, shall be UNIFORM throughout the United States."

It has been very properly observed, by different speakers and writers on the side of the constitution, that if the exercise of the power of internal taxation by the union, should be judged beforehand upon mature consideration, or should be discovered on experiment to be really inconvenient, the federal government may forbear the use of it, and have recourse to requisitions in its stead. By way of answer to this, it has been triumphantly asked, why not in the first instance omit that ambiguous power, and rely upon the latter resource? Two solid answers may be given; the first is, that the actual exercise of the power, may be found both *convenient* and *necessary;* for it is impossible to prove in theory, or otherwise than by the experiment, that it cannot be advantageously exercised. The contrary indeed, appears most probable. The second answer is, that the existence of such a power in the constitution, will have a strong influence in giving efficacy to requisitions. When the states know that the union can supply itself without their agency, it will be a powerful motive for exertion on their part.

As to the interference of the revenue laws of the union, and of its members, we have already seen that there can be no clashing or repugnancy of authority. The laws cannot, therefore, in a legal sense, interfere with each other; and it is far from impossible to avoid an interference even in the policy of their different systems. An effectual expedient for this purpose will be, mutually to abstain from those objects, which either side may have first had recourse to. As neither can *control* the other, each will have an obvious and sensible interest in this reciprocal forbearance. And where there is an *immediate* common interest, we may safely count upon its operation. When the particular debts of the states are done away, and their expenses come to be limited within their natural compass, the possibility almost of interference will vanish. A small land tax will answer the purpose of the states, and will be their most simple, and most fit resource.

Many spectres have been raised out of this power of internal taxation, to excite the apprehensions of the people . . . double sets of revenue officers . . . a duplication of their burthens by double taxations, and the frightful forms of odious and oppressive poll taxes, have been played off with all the ingenious dexterity of political legerdemain.

As to the first point, there are two cases in which there can be no room for double sets of officers; one, where the right of imposing the tax is exclusively vested in the union, which applies to the duties on imports: the other, where the object has not fallen under any state regulation or provision, which may be applicable to a variety of objects. In other cases, the probability is, that the United States will either wholly abstain from the objects pre-occupied for local purposes, or will make use of the state officers, and state regulations, for collecting the additional imposition. This will best answer the views of revenue, because it will save expense in the collection, and will best avoid any occasion of disgust to the state governments and to the people. At all events, here is a practicable expedient for avoiding such an inconvenience; and noth-

No. 36

ing more can be required than to show, that evils predicted do not necessarily result from the plan.

As to any argument derived from a supposed system of influence, it is a sufficient answer to say, that it ought not to be presumed; but the supposition is susceptible of a more precise answer. If such a spirit should infest the councils of the union, the most certain road to the accomplishment of its aim would be, to employ the state officers as much as possible, and to attach them to the union by an accumulation of their emoluments. This would serve to turn the tide of state influence into the channels of the national government, instead of making federal influence flow in an opposite and adverse current. But all suppositions of this kind are invidious, and ought to be banished from the consideration of the great question before the people. They can answer no other end than to cast a mist over the truth.

As to the suggestion of double taxation, the answer is plain. The wants of the union are to be supplied in one way or another; if by the authority of the federal government, then it will not remain to be done by that of the state governments. The quantity of taxes to be paid by the community, must be the same in either case; with this advantage, if the provision is to be made by the union . . . that the capital resource of commercial imposts, which is the most convenient branch of revenue, can be prudently improved to a much greater extent under federal, than under state regulation, and of course will render it less necessary to recur to more inconvenient methods; and with this further advantage, that as far as there may be any real difficulty in the exercise of the power of internal taxation, it will impose a disposition to greater care in the choice and arrangement of the means; and must naturally tend to make it a fixed point of policy in the national administration, to go as far as may be practicable in making the luxury of the rich tributary to the public treasury, in order to diminish the necessity of those impositions, which might create dissatisfaction in the poorer and most numerous classes of the society. Happy it is when the interest which the government has in the preservation of its own power, coincides with a proper distribution of the public burthens, and tends to guard the least wealthy part of the community from oppression!

As to poll taxes, I, without scruple, confess my disapprobation of them; and though they have prevailed from an early period in those states,* which

---

*The New England states.

have uniformly been the most tenacious of their rights, I should lament to see them introduced into practice under the national government. But does it follow, because there is a power to lay them, that they will actually be laid? Every state in the union has power to impose taxes of this kind; and yet in several of them they are unknown in practice. Are the state governments to be stigmatized as tyrannies, because they possess this power? If they are not, with what propriety can the like power justify such a charge against the national government, or even be urged as an obstacle to its adoption? As little friendly as I am to the species of imposition, I still feel a thorough conviction, that the power of having recourse to it, ought to exist in the federal government. There are certain emergencies of nations, in which expedients, that in the ordinary state of things ought to be forborn, become essential to the public weal. And the government, from the possibility of such emergencies, ought ever to have the option of making use of them. The real scarcity of objects in this country, which may be considered as productive sources of revenue, is a reason peculiar to itself, for not abridging the discretion of the national councils in this respect. There may exist certain critical and tempestuous conjunctures of the state, in which a poll tax may become an inestimable resource. And as I know nothing to exempt this portion of the globe from the common calamities that have befallen other parts of it, I acknowledge my aversion to every project that is calculated to disarm the government of a single weapon, which in any possible contingency might be usefully employed for the general defence and security.

I have now gone through the examination of those powers, proposed to be conferred upon the federal government, which relate more peculiarly to its energy, and to its efficiency for answering the great and primary objects of union. There are others which, though omitted here, will, in order to render the view of the subject more complete, be taken notice of under the next head of our inquiries. I flatter myself the progress already made, will have sufficed to satisfy the candid and judicious part of the community, that some of the objections which have been most strenuously urged against the constitution, and which were most formidable in their first appearance, are not only destitute of substance, but if they had operated in the formation of the plan, would have rendered it incompetent to the great ends of public happiness and national prosperity. I equally flatter myself, that a further and more critical investigation of the system, will serve to recommend it still more to every sincere and disinterested advocate for good government; and will leave no doubt with men of this character of the propriety and expediency of adopting it. Happy will it be for ourselves, and most honourable for human nature, if we have wisdom and virtue enough, to set so glorious an example to mankind.

PUBLIUS

No. 37

by James Madison

Concerning the difficulties which the convention must have experienced in the formation of a proper plan

In reviewing the defects of the existing confederation, and showing that they cannot be supplied by a government of less energy than that before the public, several of the most important principles of the latter fell of course under consideration. But as the ultimate object of these papers is, to determine clearly and fully the merits of this constitution, and the expediency of adopting it, our plan cannot be completed without taking a more critical and thorough survey of the work of the convention; without examining it on all its sides; comparing it in all its parts, and calculating its probable effects.

That this remaining task may be executed under impressions conducive to a just and fair result, some reflections must in this place be indulged, which candour previously suggests.

It is a misfortune, inseparable from human affairs, that public measures are rarely investigated with that spirit of moderation, which is essential to a just estimate of their real tendency to advance, or obstruct, the public good; and that this spirit is more apt to be diminished than promoted, by those occasions which require an unusual exercise of it. To those who have been led by experience to attend to this consideration, it could not appear surprising, that the act of the convention which recommends so many important changes and innovations; which may be viewed in so many lights and relations, and which touches the springs of so many passions and interests, should find or excite dispositions unfriendly, both on one side and on the other, to a fair discussion and accurate judgment of its merits. In some, it has been too evident from their own publications, that they have scanned the proposed constitution, not only with a predisposition to censure, but with a predetermination to condemn; as the language held by others, betrays an opposite predetermination or bias, which must render their opinions also of little moment in the question. In placing, however, these different characters on a level, with respect to the weight of their opinions, I wish not to insinuate that there may not be a material difference in the purity of their intentions. It is but just to remark in favour of the latter description, that as our situation is universally admitted to be peculiarly critical, and to require indispensably, that something should be done for our relief, the predetermined patron of what has been actually done, may have taken his bias from the weight of these considerations, as well as from considerations of a sinister nature. The predetermined adversary, on the other hand, can have been governed by no venial motive whatever. The intentions of the first may be upright, as they may on the contrary be culpable. The views of the last cannot be upright, and must be culpable. But the truth is, that these papers are not addressed to persons falling under either of these characters. They solicit the attention of those only, who add to a sincere zeal for the happiness of their country, a temper favourable to a just estimate of the means of promoting it.

Persons of this character will proceed to an examination of the plan submitted by the convention, not only without a disposition to find or to magnify faults; but will see the propriety of reflecting, that a faultless plan was not to be expected. Nor, will they barely make allowances for the errors which may be chargeable on the fallibility to which the convention, as a body of men, were liable; but will keep in mind, that they themselves also are but men, and ought not to assume an infallibility in rejudging the fallible opinions of others.

With equal readiness will it be perceived, that besides these inducements to candour, many allowances ought to be made, for the difficulties inherent in the very nature of the undertaking referred to the convention.

The novelty of the undertaking immediately strikes us. It has been shown in the course of these papers, that the existing confederation is founded on principles which are fallacious; that we must consequently change this first foundation, and with it, the superstructure resting upon it. It has been shown, that the other confederacies which could be consulted as precedents, have been vitiated by the same erroneous principles, and can therefore furnish no other light than that of beacons, which give warning of the course to be shunned, without pointing out that which ought to be pursued. The most that the convention could do in such a situation, was to avoid the errors suggested by the past experience of other countries, as well as of our own; and to provide a convenient mode of rectifying their own errors as future experience may unfold them.

Among the difficulties encountered by the convention, a very important one must have lain, in combining the requisite stability and energy in government, with the inviolable attention due to liberty, and to the republican form. Without substantially accomplishing this part of their undertaking, they would have very imperfectly fulfilled the object of their appointment, or the expectation of the public: yet, that it could not be easily accomplished, will be denied by no one who is unwilling to betray his ignorance of the subject. Energy in government, is essential to that security against external and internal danger, and to that prompt and salutary execution of the laws, which enter into the very definition of good government. Stability in government, is essential to national character, and to the advantages annexed to it, as well as to that repose and confidence in the minds of the people, which are among the chief blessings of civil society. An irregular and mutable legislation is not more an evil in itself, than it is odious to the people; and it may be pronounced with assurance, that the people of this country, enlightened as they are, with regard to the nature, and interested, as the great body of them are, in the effects of good government, will never be satisfied, till some remedy be applied to the vicissitudes and uncertainties, which characterize the state administrations. On comparing, however, these valuable ingredients with the vital principles of liberty, we must perceive at once, the difficulty of mingling them together in their due proportions. The genius of republican liberty, seems to demand on one side, not only that all power should be derived from the people; but, that those intrusted with it should be kept in dependence on the people, by a short duration of their appointments; and that, even during this short period, the trust should be placed not in a few, but in a number of hands. Stability, on the contrary, requires, that the hands, in which power is lodged, should continue for a length of time the same. A frequent change of men will result from a frequent return of electors; and a frequent change of measures, from a frequent change of men: whilst energy in government requires not only a certain duration of power, but the execution of it by a single hand.

How far the convention may have succeeded in this part of their work, will better appear on a more accurate view of it. From the cursory view here taken, it must clearly appear to have been an arduous part.

Not less arduous must have been the task of marking the proper line of partition, between the authority of the general, and that of the state governments. Every man will be sensible of this difficulty, in proportion as he has been accustomed to contemplate and discriminate objects, extensive and complicated in their nature. The faculties of the mind itself have never yet been distinguished and defined, with satisfactory precision, by all the efforts of the most acute and metaphysical philosophers. Sense, perception, judgment, desire, volition, memory, imagination, are found to be separated, by such delicate shades and minute gradations, that their boundaries have eluded the most subtle investigations, and remain a pregnant source of ingenious disquisition and controversy. The boundaries between the great kingdoms of nature, and still more, between the various provinces, and lesser portions, into which they are subdivided, afford another illustration of the same important truth. The most sagacious and laborious naturalists have never yet succeeded, in tracing with certainty the line which separates the district of vegetable life, from the neighbouring region of unorganized matter, or which marks the termination of the former, and the commencement of the animal empire. A still greater obscurity lies in the distinctive characters, by which the objects in each of these great departments of nature have been arranged and assorted.

When we pass from the works of nature, in which all the delineations are perfectly accurate, and appear to be otherwise only from the imperfection of the eye which surveys them, to the institutions of man, in which the obscurity arises as well from the object itself, as from the organ by which it is contemplated; we must perceive the necessity of moderating still further our expectations and hopes from the efforts of human sagacity. Experience has instructed us, that no skill in the science of government has yet been able to discriminate and define, with sufficient certainty, its three great provinces, the legislative, executive, and judiciary; or even the privileges and powers of the different legislative branches. Questions daily occur in the course of practice, which prove the obscurity which reigns in these subjects, and which puzzle the greatest adepts in political science.

The experience of ages, with the continued and combined labours of the most enlightened legislators and jurists, have been equally unsuccessful in delineating the several objects and limits of different codes of laws, and different tribunals of justice. The precise extent of the common law, the statute law, the maritime law, the ecclesiastical law, the law of corporations, and other local laws and customs, remain still to be clearly and finally established in Great Britain, where accuracy in such subjects has been more industriously pursued than in any other part of the world. The jurisdiction of her several courts, general and local, of law, of equity, of admiralty, &c. is not less a source of frequent and intricate discussions, sufficiently denoting the indeterminate limits by which they are respectively circumscribed. All new laws, though penned with the greatest technical skill, and passed on the fullest and most mature deliberation, are considered as more or less obscure and equivocal, until their meaning be liquidated and ascertained by a series of particular discussions and adjudications. Besides, the obscurity arising from the complexity of objects and the imperfection of the human faculties, the medium through which the conceptions of men are conveyed to each other, adds a fresh embarrassment. The use of words is to express ideas. Perspicuity therefore requires, not only that the ideas should be distinctly formed, but that they should be expressed by words distinctly and exclusively appropriated to them. But no language is so copious as to supply words and phrases for every complex idea, or so correct as not to include many, equivocally denoting different ideas. Hence it must happen, that however accurately objects may be discriminated in themselves, and however accurately the discrimination may be conceived, the definition of them may be rendered inaccurate, by the inaccuracy of the terms in which it is delivered. And this unavoidable inaccuracy must be greater or less, according to the complexity and novelty of the objects defined. When the Almighty himself condescends to address mankind in their own language, his meaning, luminous as it must be, is rendered dim and doubtful, by the cloudy medium through which it is communicated.

Here then are three sources of vague and incorrect definitions; indistinctness of the object, imperfection of the organ of perception, inadequateness of the vehicle of ideas. Any one of these must produce a certain degree of obscurity. The convention, in delineating the boundary between the federal and state jurisdictions, must have experienced the full effect of them all.

To the difficulties already mentioned, may be added the interfering pretensions of the larger and smaller states. We cannot err, in supposing that the former would contend for a participation in the government, fully proportioned to their superior wealth and importance; and that the latter would not be less tenacious of the equality at present enjoyed by them. We may well suppose, that neither side would entirely yield to the other, and consequently that the struggle could be terminated only by compromise. It is extremely probable also, that after the ratio of representation had been adjusted, this very compromise must have produced a fresh struggle between the same parties, to give such a turn to the organization of the government, and to the distribution of its powers, as would increase the importance of the branches, in forming which they had respectively obtained the greatest share of influence. There are features in the constitution which warrant each of these suppositions; and as far as either of them is well founded, it shows that the convention must have been compelled to sacrifice theoretical propriety, to the force of extraneous considerations.

Nor could it have been the large and small states only, which would marshal themselves in opposition to each other on various points. Other combinations, resulting from a difference of local position and policy, must have created additional difficulties. As every state may be divided into different districts, and its citizens into different classes, which give birth to contending interests and local jealousies: so the different parts of the United States are distinguished from each other, by a variety of circumstances, which produce a like effect on a larger scale. And although this variety of interests, for reasons sufficiently explained in a former paper, may have a salutary influence on the administration of the government when formed; yet every one must be sensible of the contrary influence, which must have been experienced in the task of forming it.

Would it be wonderful if, under the pressure of all these difficulties, the convention should have been forced into some deviations from that artificial structure and regular symmetry, which an abstract view of the subject might lead an ingenious theorist to bestow on a constitution planned in his closet, or in his imagination? The real wonder is, that so many difficulties should have been surmounted; and surmounted with an unanimity almost as unprecedented, as it must have been unexpected. It is impossible for any man of candour to reflect on this circumstance, without partaking of the astonishment. It is impossible, for the man of pious reflection, not to perceive in it a finger of that Almighty Hand, which has been so frequently and signally extended to our relief in the critical stages of the revolution.

We had occasion in a former paper, to take notice of the repeated trials which have been unsuccessfully made in the United Netherlands, for reforming the baneful and notorious vices of their constitution. The history of almost all the great councils and consultations, held among mankind for reconciling their discordant opinions, assuaging their mutual jealousies, and adjusting their respective interests, is a history of factions, contentions, and disappointments; and may be classed among the most dark and degrading pictures, which display the infirmities and depravities of the human character. If, in a few scattered instances, a brighter aspect is presented, they serve only as exceptions to admonish us of the general truth; and by their lustre to darken the gloom of the adverse prospect to which they are contrasted. In revolving the causes from which these exceptions result, and applying them to the particular instance before us, we are necessarily led to two important conclusions. The first is, that the convention must have enjoyed in a very singular degree, an exemption from the pestilential influence of party animosities; the diseases most incident to deliberative bodies, and most apt to contaminate their proceedings. The second conclusion is, that all the deputations composing the convention, were either satisfactorily accommodated by the final act; or were induced to accede to it, by a deep conviction of the necessity of sacrificing private opinions and partial interests to the public good; and by a despair of seeing this necessity diminished by delays or by new experiments.

PUBLIUS

No. 38

by James Madison

*The subject continued, and the incoherence
of the objections to the plan, exposed*

It is not a little remarkable, that in every case reported by ancient history, in which government has been established with deliberation and consent, the task of framing it has not been committed to an assembly of men; but has been performed by some individual citizen, of pre-eminent wisdom and approved integrity.

Minos, we learn, was the primitive founder of the government of Crete; as Zaleucus was of that of the Locrians. Theseus first, and after him Draco and Solon, instituted the government of Athens. Lycurgus was the lawgiver of Sparta. The foundation of the original government of Rome was laid by Romulus; and the work completed by two of his elective successors, Numa, and Tullus Hostilius. On the abolition of royalty, the consular administration was substituted by Brutus, who stepped forward with a project for such a reform, which he alleged had been prepared by Servius Tullius, and to which his address obtained the assent and ratification of the senate and people. This remark is applicable to confederate governments also. Amphyction, we are told, was the author of that which bore his name. The Achaean league received its first birth from Achaeus, and its second from Aratus.

What degree of agency these reputed lawgivers might have in their respective establishments, or how far they might be clothed with the legitimate authority of the people, cannot, in every instance, be ascertained. In some, however, the proceeding was strictly regular. Draco appears to have been intrusted by the people of Athens, with indefinite powers to reform its government and laws. And Solon, according to Plutarch, was in a manner compelled, by the universal suffrage of his fellow citizens, to take upon him the sole and absolute power of new modelling the constitution. The proceedings under Lycurgus were less regular: but as far as the advocates for a regular reform could prevail, they all turned their eyes towards the single efforts of that celebrated patriot and sage, instead of seeking to bring about a revolution, by the intervention of a deliberative body of citizens.

Whence could it have proceeded, that a people, jealous as the Greeks were of their liberty, should so far abandon the rules of caution as to place their destiny in the hands of a single citizen? Whence could it have proceeded that the Athenians, a people who would not suffer an army to be commanded by fewer than ten generals, and who required no other proof of danger to their liberties than the illustrious merit of a fellow citizen, should consider one illustrious citizen as a more eligible despository of the fortunes of themselves and their posterity, than a select body of citizens, from whose common deliberations more wisdom, as well as more safety, might have been expected? These questions cannot be fully answered, without supposing that the fears of discord and disunion among a number of counsellors, exceeded the apprehension of treachery or incapacity in a single individual. History informs us likewise, of the difficulties with which these celebrated reformers had to contend; as well as of the expedients which they were obliged to employ, in order to carry their reforms into effect. Solon, who seems to have indulged a more temporizing policy, confessed that he had not given to his countrymen the government best suited to their happiness, but most tolerable to their prejudices. And Lycurgus, more true to his object, was under the necessity of mixing a portion of violence with the authority of superstition; and of securing his final success, by a voluntary renunciation, first of his country, and then of his life.

If these lessons teach us, on one hand, to admire the improvement made by America on the ancient mode of preparing and establishing regular plans of government; they serve not less on the other, to admonish us of the hazards and difficulties incident to such experiments, and of the great imprudence of unnecessarily multiplying them.

Is it an unreasonable conjecture, that the errors which may be contained in the plan of the convention, are such as have resulted, rather from the defect of antecedent experience on this complicated and difficult subject, than from a want of accuracy or care in the investigation of it; and consequently, such as will not be ascertained until an actual trial shall have pointed them out? This conjecture is rendered probable, not only by many considerations of a general nature, but by the particular case of the articles of confederation.

It is observable, that among the numerous objections and amendments suggested by the several states, when these articles were submitted for their ratification, not one is found, which alludes to the great and radical error, which on actual trial has discovered itself. And if we except the observations which New Jersey was led to make rather by her local situation, than by her peculiar foresight, it may be questioned whether a single suggestion was of sufficient moment to justify a revision of the system. There is abundant reason nevertheless to suppose, that immaterial as these objections were, they would have been adhered to with a very dangerous inflexibility in some states, had not a zeal for their opinions and supposed interests, been stifled by the more powerful sentiment of self-preservation. One state, we may remember, persisted for several years in refusing her concurrence, although the enemy remained the whole period at our gates, or rather in the very bowels of our country. Nor was her pliancy in the end effected by a less motive, than the fear of being chargeable with protracting the public calamities, and endangering the event of the contest. Every candid reader will make the proper reflections on these important facts.

A patient, who finds his disorder daily growing worse, and that an efficacious remedy can no longer be delayed without extreme danger; after coolly revolving his situation, and the characters of different physicians, selects and calls in such of them as he judges most capable of administering relief, and best entitled to his confidence. The physicians attend: the case of the patient is carefully examined . . . a consultation is held: they are unanimously agreed that the symptoms are critical; but that the case, with proper and timely relief, is so far from being desperate, that it may be made to issue in an improvement of his constitution. They are equally unanimous in prescribing the remedy by which this happy effect is to be produced. The prescription is no sooner made known, however, than a number of persons interpose, and without denying the reality or danger of the disorder, assure the patient that the prescription will be poison to his constitution, and forbid him, under pain of certain death, to make use of it. Might not the patient reasonably demand, before he ventured to follow this advice, that the authors of it should at least agree among themselves, on some other remedy to be substituted? And if he found them differing as much from one another, as from

No. 38

his first counsellors, would he not act prudently, in trying the experiment unanimously recommended by the latter, rather than in hearkening to those who could neither deny the necessity of a speedy remedy, nor agree in proposing one.

Such a patient, and in such a situation, is America at this moment. She has been sensible of her malady. She has obtained a regular and unanimous advice from men of her own deliberate choice. And she is warned by others against following this advice, under pain of the most fatal consequences. Do the monitors deny the reality of her danger? No. Do they deny the necessity of some speedy and powerful remedy? No. Are they agreed, are any two of them agreed, in their objections to the remedy proposed, or in the proper one to be substituted? Let them speak for themselves.

This one tells us, that the proposed constitution ought to be rejected, because it is not a confederation of the states, but a government over individuals. Another admits, that it ought to be a government over individuals, to a certain extent, but by no means to the extent proposed. A third does not object to the government over individuals, or to the extent proposed, but to the want of a bill of rights. A fourth concurs in the absolute necessity of a bill of rights, but contends that it ought to be declaratory, not of the personal rights of individuals, but of the rights reserved to the states in their political capacity. A fifth is of opinion that a bill of rights of any sort would be superfluous and misplaced, and that the plan would be unexceptionable, but for the fatal power of regulating the times and places of election. An objector in a large state, exclaims loudly against the unreasonable equality of representation in the senate. An objector in a small state, is equally loud against the dangerous inequality in the house of representatives. From this quarter, we are alarmed with the amazing expense, from the number of persons who are to administer the new government. From another quarter, and sometimes from the same quarter, on another occasion, the cry is, that the congress will be but the shadow of a representation, and that the government would be far less objectionable, if the number and the expense were doubled. A patriot in a state that does not import or export, discerns insuperable objections against the power of direct taxation. The patriotic adversary in a state of great exports and imports, is not less dissatisfied that the whole burthen of taxes may be thrown on consumption. This politician discovers in the constitution a direct and irresistible tendency to monarchy: that, is equally sure, it will end in aristocracy. Another is puzzled to say which of these shapes it will ultimately assume, but sees clearly it must be one or other of them. Whilst a fourth is not wanting, who with no less confidence affirms, that the constitution is so far from having a bias towards either of these dangers, that the weight on that side will not be sufficient to keep it upright and firm against its opposite propensities. With another class of adversaries to the constitution, the language is, that the legislative, executive, and judiciary departments, are intermixed in such a manner, as to contradict all the ideas of regular government, and all the requisite precautions in favor of liberty. Whilst this objection circulates in vague and general expressions, there are not a few who lend their sanction to it. Let each one come forward with his particular explanation, and scarcely any two are exactly agreed on the subject. In the eyes of one, the junction of the senate with the president, in the responsible function of appointing to offices, instead of vesting this executive power in the executive alone, is the vicious part of the organization. To another, the exclusion of the house of representatives, whose numbers alone could be a due security against corruption and partiality in the exercise of such a power, is equally obnoxious. With another, the admission of the president into any share of a power, which must ever be a dangerous engine in the hands of the executive magistrate, is an unpardonable violation of the maxims of republican jealousy. No part of the arrangement, according to some, is more inadmissible than the trial of impeachments by the senate, which is alternately a member both of the legislative and executive departments, when this power so evidently belonged to the judiciary department. We concur fully, reply others, in the objection to this part of the plan, but we can never agree that a reference of impeachments to the judiciary authority would be an amendment of the error: our principal dislike to the organization, arises from the extensive powers already lodged in that department. Even among the zealous patrons of a council of state, the most irreconcileable variance is discovered, concerning the mode in which it ought to be constituted. The demand of one gentleman is, that the council should consist of a small number, to be appointed by the most numerous branch of the legislature. Another would prefer a larger number, and considers it as a fundamental condition, that the appointment should be made by the president himself.

As it can give no umbrage to the writers against the plan of the federal constitution, let us suppose, that as they are the most zealous, so they are also the most sagacious, of those who think the late convention were unequal to the task assigned them, and that a wiser and better plan might and ought to be substituted. Let us further suppose, that their country should concur, both in this favourable opinion of their merits, and in their unfavourable opinion of the convention; and should accordingly proceed to form them into a second convention, with full powers, and for the express purpose, of revising and remoulding the work of the first. Were the experiment to be seriously made, though it requires some effort to view it seriously even in fiction, I leave it to be decided by the sample of opinions just exhibited, whether, with all their enmity to their predecessors, they would, in any one point, depart so widely from their example, as in the discord and ferment that would mark their own deliberations; and whether the constitution, now before the public, would not stand as fair a chance for immortality, as Lycurgus gave to that of Sparta, by making its change to depend on his own return from exile and death, if it were to be immediately adopted, and were to continue in force, not until a BETTER, but until ANOTHER should be agreed upon by this new assembly of lawgivers.

It is a matter both of wonder and regret, that those who raise so many objections against the new constitution, should never call to mind the defects of that which is to be exchanged for it. It is not necessary that the former should be perfect: it is sufficient that the latter is more imperfect. No man would refuse to give brass for silver or gold, because the latter had some alloy in it. No man would refuse to quit a shattered and tottering habitation, for a firm and commodious building, because the latter had not a porch to it; or because some of the rooms might be a little larger or smaller, or the cieling a little higher or lower than his fancy would have planned them. But wa[i]ving illustrations of this sort, is it not manifest, that most of the capital objections urged against the new system, lie with tenfold weight against the existing confederation? Is an indefinite power to raise money, dangerous in the hands of a federal government? The present congress can make requisitions to any amount they please; and the states are constitutionally bound to furnish them. They can emit bills of credit as long as they will pay for the paper: they can borrow both abroad and at home, as long as a shilling will be lent. Is an indefinite power to raise troops dangerous? The confederation gives to congress that power also; and they have already begun to make use of it. Is it improper and unsafe to intermix the different powers of government in the same body of men? Congress, a single body of men, are the sole depository of all the federal powers. Is it particularly dangerous to give the keys of the treasury, and the command of the army, into the same hands? The confederation places them both in the hands of congress. Is a bill of rights essential to liberty? The confederation has no bill of rights. Is it an objection against the new constitution, that it empowers the senate, with the concurrence of the executive, to make treaties which are to be the laws of the land? The existing congress, without any such control, can make treaties which they themselves have declared, and most of the states have recognized, to be the supreme law of the land. Is the importation of slaves permitted by the new constitution for twenty years? By the old it is permitted for ever.

I shall be told, that however dangerous this mixture of powers may be in theory, it is rendered harmless by the dependence of congress on the states for the means of carrying them into practice; that, however large the mass of powers may be, it is in fact a lifeless mass. Then, say I, in the first place, that the confederation is chargeable with the still greater folly, of declaring certain powers in the federal government to be absolutely necessary, and at the same time rendering them absolutely nugatory; and, in the next place, that if the union is to continue, and no better government be substituted, effective powers must either be granted to, or assumed by, the existing congress; in either of which events, the contrast just stated will hold good. But this is not all. Out of this lifeless mass, has already grown an excrescent power, which tends to realize all the dangers that can be apprehended from a defective construction of the supreme government of the union. It is now no longer a point of speculation and hope, that the western territory is a mine of vast wealth to the United States; and although it is not of such a nature as to extricate them from their present distresses, or for some time to come to yield any regular supplies for the public expenses; yet must it hereafter be able, under proper management, both to effect a gradual discharge of the domestic debt, and to furnish, for a certain period, liberal tributes to the federal treasury. A very large proportion of this fund has been already surrendered by individual states; and it may with reason be expected, that the remaining states will not persist in withholding similar proofs of their equity and generosity. We may calculate, therefore, that a rich and fertile country, of an area equal to the inhabited extent of the United States, will soon become a national stock. Congress have assumed the administration of this stock. They have begun to render it productive. Congress have undertaken to do more:... they have proceeded to form new states; to erect temporary governments; to appoint officers for them; and to prescribe the conditions on which such states shall be admitted into the confederacy. All this has been done; and done without the least colour of constitutional authority. Yet no blame has been whispered: no alarm has been sounded. A GREAT and INDEPENDENT fund of revenue is passing into the hands of a SINGLE BODY of men, who can RAISE TROOPS to an INDEFINITE NUMBER, and appropriate money to their support for an INDEFINITE PERIOD OF TIME. And yet there are men, who have not only been silent spectators of this prospect, but who are advocates for the system which exhibits it; and, at the same time, urge against the new system the objections which we have heard. Would they not act with more consistency, in urging the establishment of the latter, as no less necessary to guard the union against the future powers and resources of a body constructed like the existing congress, than to save it from the dangers threatened by the present impotency of that assembly?

I mean not, by any thing here said, to throw censure on the measures which have been pursued by congress. I am sensible they could not have done otherwise. The public interest, the necessity of the case, imposed upon them the task of overleaping their constitutional limits. But is not the fact an alarming proof of the danger resulting from a government, which does not possess regular powers commensurate to its objects? A dissolution, or usurpation, is the dreadful dilemma to which it is continually exposed.

PUBLIUS

No. 39

by James Madison

The conformity of the plan to republican principles: an objection in respect to the powers of the convention, examined

The last paper having concluded the observations, which were meant to introduce a candid survey of the plan of government reported by the convention, we now proceed to the execution of that part of our undertaking.

The first question that offers itself is, whether the general form and aspect of the government be strictly republican? It is evident that no other form would be reconcileable with the genius of the people of America; with the fundamental principles of the revolution; or with that honourable determination which animates every votary of freedom, to rest all our political experiments on the capacity of mankind for self-government. If the plan of the convention, therefore, be found to depart from the republican character, its advocates must abandon it as no longer defensible.

What then are the distinctive characters of the republican form? Were an answer to this question to be sought, not by recurring to principles, but in the application of the term by political writers, to the constitutions of different states, no satisfactory one would ever be found. Holland, in which no particle of the supreme authority is derived from the people, has passed almost universally under the denomination of a republic. The same title has been bestowed on Venice, where absolute power over the great body of the people is exercised, in the most absolute manner, by a small body of hereditary nobles. Poland, which is a mixture of aristocracy and of monarchy in their worst forms, has been dignified with the same appellation. The government of England, which has one republican branch only, combined with a hereditary aristocracy and monarchy, has, with equal impropriety, been frequently placed on the list of republics. These examples, which are nearly as dissimilar to each other as to a genuine republic, show the extreme inaccuracy with which the term has been used in political disquisitions.

If we resort for a criterion, to the different principles on which different forms of government are established, we may define a republic to be, or at least may bestow that name on, a government which derives all its powers directly or indirectly from the great body of the people; and is administered by persons holding their offices during pleasure, for a limited period, or during good behaviour. It is *essential* to such a government, that it be derived from the great body of the society, not from an inconsiderable proportion, or a favoured class of it; otherwise a handful of tyrannical nobles, exercising their oppressions by a delegation of their powers, might aspire to the rank of republicans, and claim for their government the honourable title of republic. It is *sufficient* for such a government, that the persons administering it be appointed, either directly or indirectly, by the people; and that they hold their appointments by either of the tenures just specified; otherwise every government in the United States, as well as every other popular government that has been, or can be well organized or well executed, would be degraded from the republican character. According to the constitution of every state in the union, some or other of the officers of government are appointed indirectly only by the people. According to most of them, the chief magistrate himself is so appointed. And according to one, this mode of appointment is extended to one of the co-ordinate branches of the legislature. According to all the constitutions also, the tenure of the highest offices is extended to a definite period, and in many instances, both within the legislative and executive departments, to a period of years. According to the provisions of most of the constitutions, again, as well as according to the most respectable and received opinions on the subject, the members of the judiciary department are to retain their offices by the firm tenure of good behaviour.

On comparing the constitution planned by the convention, with the standard here fixed, we perceive at once, that it is, in the most rigid sense, conformable to it. The house of representatives, like that of one branch at least of all the state legislatures, is elected immediately by the great body of the people. The senate, like the present congress, and the senate of Maryland, derives its appointment indirectly from the people. The president is indirectly derived from the choice of the people, according to the example in most of the states. Even the judges, with all other officers of the union, will, as in the several states, be the choice, though a remote choice, of the people themselves. The duration of the appointments is equally conformable to the republican standard, and to the model of the state constitutions. The house of representatives is periodically elective, as in all the states; and for the period of two years, as in the state of South Carolina. The senate is elective, for the period of six years; which is but one year more than the period of the senate of Maryland; and but two more than that of the senates of New York and Virginia. The president is to continue in office for the period of four years; as in New York and Delaware, the chief magistrate is elected for three years, and in South Carolina for two years. In the other states the election is annual. In several of the states, however, no explicit provision is made for the impeachment of the chief magistrate. And in Delaware and Virginia, he is not impeachable till out of office. The president of the United States is impeachable at any time during his continuance in office. The tenure by which the judges are to hold their places, is, as it unquestionably ought to be, that of good behaviour. The tenure of the ministerial offices generally, will be a subject of legal regulation, conformably to the reason of the case, and the example of the state constitutions.

Could any further proof be required of the republican complexion of this system, the most decisive one might be found in its absolute prohibition of titles of nobility, both under the federal and the state governments; and in its express guarantee of the republican form to each of the latter.

But it was not sufficient, say the adversaries of the proposed constitution, for the convention to adhere to the republican form. They ought, with equal care, to have preserved the *federal* form, which regards the union as a *confederacy* of sovereign states; instead of which, they have framed a *national* government, which regards the union as a *consolidation* of the states. And it is asked, by what authority this bold and radical innovation was undertaken? The handle which has been made of this objection requires, that it should be examined with some precision.

Without inquiring into the accuracy of the distinction on which the objection is founded, it will be necessary to a just estimate of its force, first, to ascertain the real character of the government in question; secondly, to inquire how far the convention were authorized to propose such a government; and thirdly, how far the duty they owed to their country, could supply any defect of regular authority.

First. In order to ascertain the real character of the government, it may be considered in relation to the foundation on which it is to be established; to the sources from which its ordinary powers are to be drawn; to the operation of those powers; to the extent of them; and to the authority by which future changes in the government are to be introduced.

On examining the first relation, it appears, on one hand, that the constitution is to be founded on the assent and ratification of the people of America, given by deputies elected for the special purpose; but on the other, that this assent and ratification is to be given by the people, not as individuals composing one entire nation, but as composing the distinct and independent states to which they respectively belong. It is to be the assent and ratification of the several states, derived from the supreme authority in each state ... the authority of the people themselves. The act, therefore, establishing the constitution, will not be a *national*, but a *federal* act.

That it will be a federal, and not a national act, as these terms are understood by the objectors, the act of the people, as forming so many independent states, not as forming one aggregate nation, is obvious from this single consideration, that it is to result neither from the decision of a *majority* of the people of the union, nor from that of a *majority* of the states. It must result from the *unanimous* assent of the several states that are parties to it, differing no otherwise from their ordinary assent than in its being expressed, not by the legislative authority, but by that of the people themselves. Were the people regarded in this transaction as forming one nation, the will of the majority of the whole people of the United States would bind the minority; in the same manner as the majority in each state must bind the minority; and the will of the majority must be determined either by a comparison of the individual votes, or by considering the will of the majority of the states, as evidence of the will of a majority of the people of the United States. Neither of these rules has been adopted. Each state, in ratifying the constitution, is considered as a sovereign body, independent of all others, and only to be bound by its own voluntary act. In this relation, then, the new constitution will, if established, be a *federal*, and not a *national* constitution.

The next relation is, to the sources from which the ordinary powers of government are to be derived. The house of representatives will derive its powers from the people of America, and the people will be represented in the same proportion, and on the same principle, as they are in the legislature of a particular state. So far the government is *national*, not *federal*. The senate, on the other hand, will derive its powers from the states, as political and co-equal societies; and these will be represented on the principle of equality in the senate, as they now are in the existing congress. So far the government is *federal*, not *national*. The executive power will be derived from a very compound source. The immediate election of the president is to be made by the states in their political characters. The votes allotted to them are in a compound ratio, which considers them partly as distinct and co-equal societies; partly as unequal members of the same society. The eventual election, again, is to be made by that branch of the legislature which consists of the national representatives; but in this particular act, they are to be thrown into the form of individual delegations from so many distinct and co-equal bodies politic. From this aspect of the government, it appears to be of a mixed character, presenting at least as many *federal* as *national* features.

The difference between a federal and national government, as it relates to the *operation of the government*, is, by the adversaries of the plan of the convention, supposed to consist in this, that in the former, the powers operate on the political bodies composing the confederacy, in their political capacities; in the latter, on the individual citizens composing the nation, in their individual capacities. On trying the constitution by this criterion, it falls under the *national*, not the *federal* character; though perhaps not so completely as has been understood. In several cases, and particularly in the trial of controversies to which states may be parties, they must be viewed and proceeded against in their collective and political capacities only. But the operation of the government on the people in their individual capacities, in its ordinary and most essential proceedings, will, on the whole, in the sense of its opponents, designate it in this relation, a *national* government.

But if the government be national, with regard to the *operation* of its powers, it changes its aspect again, when we contemplate it in relation to the *extent* of its powers. The idea of a national government involves in it, not only an authority over the individual citizens, but an indefinite supremacy over all persons and things, so far as they are objects of lawful government. Among a people consolidated into one nation, this supremacy is completely vested in the national legislature. Among communities united for particular purposes, it is vested partly in the general, and partly in the municipal legislatures. In the former case, all local authorities are subordinate to the supreme; and may be controled, directed, or abolished by it at pleasure. In the latter, the local or municipal authorities form distinct and independent portions of the supremacy, no more subject, within their respective spheres, to the general authority, than the general authority is subject to them within its own sphere. In this relation, then, the proposed government cannot be deemed a *national* one; since its jurisdiction extends to certain enumerated objects only, and leaves to the several states, a residuary and inviolable sovereignty over all other objects. It is true, that in controversies relating to the boundary between the two jurisdictions, the tribunal which is ultimately to decide, is to be established under the general government. But this does not change the principle of the case. The decision is to be impartially made, according to the rules of the constitution: and all the usual and most effectual precautions are taken to secure this impartiality. Some such tribunal is clearly essential to prevent an appeal to the sword, and a dissolution of the compact; and that it ought to be established under the general, rather than under the local governments; or, to speak more properly, that it could be safely established under the first alone, is a position not likely to be combated.

If we try the constitution by its last relation, to the authority by which amendments are to be made, we find it neither wholly *national*, nor wholly *federal*. Were it wholly national, the supreme and ultimate authority would reside in the majority of the people of the union; and this authority would be competent at all times, like that of a majority of every national society, to alter or abolish its established government. Were it wholly federal on the other hand, the concurrence of each state in the union would be essential to every alteration that would be binding on all. The mode provided by the plan of the convention, is not founded on either of these principles. In requiring more than a majority, and particularly, in computing the proportion by *states*, not by *citizens*, it departs from the *national*, and advances towards the *federal* character. In rendering the concurrence of less than the whole number of states sufficient, it loses again the *federal*, and partakes of the *national* character.

The proposed constitution, therefore, even when tested by the rules laid down by its antagonists, is, in strictness, neither a national nor a federal constitution; but a composition of both. In its foundation it is federal, not national; in the sources from which the ordinary powers of the government are drawn, it is partly federal, and partly national; in the operation of these powers, it is national, not federal; in the extent of them again, it is federal, not national; and finally, in the authoritative mode of introducing amendments, it is neither wholly federal, nor wholly national.

PUBLIUS

No. 40

by James Madison

The same objection further examined

The *second* point to be examined is, whether the convention were authorized to frame, and propose this mixed constitution.

The powers of the convention ought, in strictness, to be determined, by an inspection of the commissions given to the members by their respective constituents. As all of these, however, had reference, either to the recommendation from the meeting at Annapolis, in September, 1786, or to that from congress, in February, 1787, it will be sufficient to recur to these particular acts.

The act from Annapolis recommends the "appointment of commissioners to take into consideration the situation of the United States; to devise *such further provisions,* as shall appear to them necessary to render the constitution of the federal government, *adequate to the exigencies of the union;* and to report such an act for that purpose, to the United States in congress assembled, as, when agreed to by them, and afterwards confirmed by the legislature of every state, will effectually provide for the same."

The recommendatory act of congress is in the words following: "Whereas, there is provision in the articles of confederation and perpetual union, for making alterations therein, by the assent of a congress of the United States, and of the legislatures of the several states; and whereas experience hath evinced, that there are defects in the present confederation; as a mean to remedy which, several of the states, and *particularly the state of New York,* by express instructions to their delegates in congress, have suggested a convention for the purposes expressed in the following resolution; and such convention appearing to be the most probable mean of establishing in these states, *a firm national government:*

"Resolved, That in the opinion of congress, it is expedient, that on the 2d Monday in May next, a convention of delegates, who shall have been appointed by the several states, be held at Philadelphia, for the sole and express purpose *of revising the articles of confederation,* and reporting to congress and the several legislatures, such *alterations and provisions therein,* as shall, when agreed to in congress, and confirmed by the states, render the federal constitution *adequate to the exigencies of government, and the preservation of the union.*"

From these two acts, it appears, 1st, that the object of the convention was to establish, in these states, *a firm national government;* 2d, that this government was to be such as would be *adequate to the exigencies of government,* and *the preservation of the union;* 3d, that these purposes were to be effected by *alterations and provisions in the articles of confederation,* as it is expressed in the act of congress; or by *such further provisions as should appear necessary,* as it stands in the recommendatory act from Annapolis; 4th. that the alterations and provisions were to be reported to congress, and to the states, in order to be agreed to by the former, and confirmed by the latter.

No. 40

From a comparison, and fair construction, of these several modes of expression, is to be deduced the authority under which the convention acted. They were to frame a *national government,* adequate to the *exigencies of government,* and *of the union;* and to reduce the articles of confederation into such form, as to accomplish these purposes.

There are two rules of construction, dictated by plain reason, as well as founded on legal axioms. The one is, that every part of the expression ought, if possible, to be allowed some meaning, and be made to conspire to some common end. The other is, that where the several parts cannot be made to coincide, the less important should give way to the more important part: the means should be sacrificed to the end, rather than the end to the means.

Suppose, then, that the expressions defining the authority of the convention, were irreconcileably at variance with each other; that a *national* and *adequate government* could not possibly, in the judgment of the convention, be effected by *alterations* and *provisions* in the *articles of confederation;* which part of the definition ought to have been embraced, and which rejected? Which was the more important; which the less important part? Which the end; which the means? Let the most scrupulous expositors of delegated powers; let the most inveterate objectors against those exercised by the convention, answer these questions. Let them declare, whether it was of most importance to the happiness of the people of America, that the articles of confederation should be disregarded, and an adequate government be provided, and the union preserved; or that an adequate government should be omitted, and the articles of confederation preserved. Let them declare, whether the preservation of these articles was the end, for securing which a reform of the government was to be introduced as the means; or whether the establishment of a government, adequate to the national happiness, was the end at which these articles themselves originally aimed, and to which they ought, as insufficient means, to have been sacrificed.

But is it necessary to suppose, that these expressions are absolutely irreconcileable to each other; that no *alterations* or *provisions* in the *articles of the confederation,* could possibly mould them into a national and adequate government; into such a government as has been proposed by the convention?

No stress, it is presumed, will, in this case, be laid on the *title;* a change of that could never be deemed an exercise of ungranted power. *Alterations* in the body of the instrument are expressly authorized. *New provisions* therein are also expressly authorized. Here then is a power to change the title; to insert new articles; to alter old ones. Must it of necessity be admitted, that this power is infringed, so long as a part of the old articles remain? Those who maintain the affirmative, ought at least to mark the boundary between authorized and usurped innovations; between that degree of change which lies within the compass of *alterations and further provisions,* and that which amounts to a *transmutation* of the government. Will it be said, that the alterations ought not to have touched the substance of the confederation? The states would never have appointed a convention with so much solemnity, nor described its objects with so much latitude, if some *substantial* reform had not been in contemplation. Will it be said, that the *fundamental principles* of the confederation were not within the purview of the convention, and ought not to have been varied? I ask, what are these principles? Do they require, that in the establishment of the constitution, the states should be regarded as distinct and independent sovereigns? They are so regarded by the constitution proposed. Do they require, that the members of the government should derive their appointment from the legislatures, not from the people of the states? One branch of the new government is to be appointed by these legislatures; and under the confederation, the delegates to congress *may all* be appointed immediately by the people; and in two states* are actually so appointed. Do they require, that the powers of the government should act on the states, and not immediately on individuals? In some instances, as has been shown, the powers of the new government will act on the states in their collective characters. In some instances also, those of the existing government act immediately on individuals. In cases of capture; of piracy; of the post-office; of coins, weights, and measures; of trade with the Indians; of claims under grants of land, by different states; and, above all, in the case of trials by courts martial in the army and navy, by which death may be inflicted without the intervention of a jury, or even of a civil magistrate: in all these cases, the powers of the confederation operate immediately on the persons and interests of individual citizens. Do these fundamental principles require, particularly, that no tax should be levied, without the intermediate agency of the states? The confederation itself, authorizes a direct tax, to a certain extent, on the post-office. The power of coinage, has been so construed by congress,

---

*Connecticut and Rhode Island.

as to levy a tribute immediately from that source also. But, pretermitting these instances, was it not an acknowledged object of the convention, and the universal expectation of the people, that the regulation of trade should be submitted to the general government, in such a form as would render it an immediate source of general revenue? Had not congress repeatedly recommended this measure, as not inconsistent with the fundamental principles of the confederation? Had not every state, but one; had not New York herself, so far complied with the plan of congress, as to recognize the *principle* of the innovation? Do these principles, in fine, require that the powers of the general government should be limited, and that, beyond this limit, the states should be left in possession of their sovereignty and independence? We have seen that, in the new government, as in the old, the general powers are limited; and that the states, in all unenumerated cases, are left in the enjoyment of their sovereign and independent jurisdiction.

The truth is, that the great principles of the constitution proposed by the convention, may be considered less, as absolutely new, than as the expansion of principles which are found in the articles of confederation. The misfortune under the latter system has been, that these principles are so feeble and confined, as to justify all the charges of inefficiency which have been urged against it; and to require a degree of enlargement, which gives to the new system the aspect of an entire transformation of the old.

In one particular, it is admitted, that the convention have departed from the tenor of their commission. Instead of reporting a plan requiring the confirmation *of all the states,* they have reported a plan, which is to be confirmed, and may be carried into effect, by *nine states only.* It is worthy of remark, that this objection, though the most plausible, has been the least urged in the publications which have swarmed against the convention. The forbearance can only have proceeded from an irresistible conviction of the absurdity of subjecting the fate of twelve states to the perverseness or corruption of a thirteenth; from the example of inflexible opposition given by a *majority* of one sixtieth of the people of America, to a measure approved and called for by the voice of twelve states, comprising fifty-nine sixtieths of the people; an example still fresh in the memory and indignation of every citizen who has felt for the wounded honour and prosperity of his country. As this objection, therefore, has been in a manner waved by those who have criticised the powers of the convention, I dismiss it without further observation.

The *third* point to be inquired into is, how far considerations of duty arising out of the case itself, could have supplied any defect of regular authority.

In the preceding inquiries, the powers of the convention have been analyzed and tried with the same rigour, and by the same rules, as if they had been real and final powers, for the establishment of a constitution for the United States. We have seen, in what manner they have borne the trial, even on that supposition. It is time now to recollect, that the powers were merely advisory and recommendatory; that they were so meant by the states, and so understood by the convention; and that the latter have accordingly planned and proposed a constitution, which is to be of no more consequence than the paper on which it is written, unless it be stamped with the approbation of those to whom it is addressed. This reflection places the subject in a point of view altogether different, and will enable us to judge with propriety of the course taken by the convention.

Let us view the ground on which the convention stood. It may be collected from their proceedings, that they were deeply and unanimously impressed with the crisis, which had led their country, almost with one voice, to make so singular and solemn an experiment, for correcting the errors of a system, by which this crisis had been produced; that they were no less deeply and unanimously convinced, that such a reform as they have proposed, was absolutely necessary to effect the purposes of their appointment. It could not be unknown to them, that the hopes and expectations of the great body of citizens, throughout this great empire, were turned with the keenest anxiety, to the event of their deliberations. They had every reason to believe, that the contrary sentiments agitated the minds and bosoms of every external and internal foe to the liberty and prosperity of the United States. They had seen in the origin and progress of the experiment, the alacrity with which the *proposition,* made by a single state (Virginia) towards a partial amendment of the confederation, had been attended to and promoted. They had seen the *liberty assumed* by a *very few* deputies, from a *very few* states, convened at Annapolis, of recommending a great and critical object, wholly foreign to their commission, not only justified by the public opinion, but actually carried into effect, by twelve out of the thirteen states. They had seen, in a variety of instances, assumptions by congress, not only of recommendatory, but of operative powers, warranted in the public estimation, by occasions and objects infinitely less urgent than those by which their conduct was to be governed. They must have reflected, that in all great changes of established governments, forms ought to give way to substance; that a rigid adherence in such cases to the former, would render nominal and nugatory, the transcendent and precious right of the people to "abolish or alter their governments as to them shall seem most likely to effect their safety and happiness;"* since it is impossible for the people spontaneously and universally, to move in concert towards their object: and it is therefore essential, that such changes be instituted by some *informal and unauthorized propositions,* made by some patriotic and respectable citizen, or number of citizens. They must have recollected, that it was by this irregular and assumed privilege, of proposing to the people plans for their safety and happiness, that the states were first united against the danger with which they were threatened by their ancient government; that committees and congresses were formed for concentrating their efforts, and defencing their rights; and that *conventions* were *elected* in *the several states,* for establishing the constitutions under which they are now governed. Nor could it have been forgotten, that no little illtimed scruples, no zeal for adhering to ordinary forms, were any where seen, except in those who wished to indulge, under these masks, their secret enmity to the substance contended for. They must have borne in mind, that as the plan to be framed and proposed, was to be submitted to *the people themselves,* the disapprobation of this supreme authority would destroy it for ever: its approbation blot out all antecedent errors and irregularities. It might even have occurred to them, that where a disposition to cavil prevailed, their neglect to execute the degree of power vested in them, and still more their recommendation of any measure whatever not warranted by their commission, would not less excite animadversion, than a recommendation at once of a measure fully commensurate to the national exigencies.

Had the convention, under all these impressions, and in the midst of all these considerations, instead of exercising a manly confidence in their country, by whose confidence they had been so peculiarly distinguished, and of pointing out a system capable, in their judgment, of securing its happiness, taken the cold and sullen resolution of disappointing its ardent hopes, of sacrificing substance to forms, of committing the dearest interests of their country to the uncertainties of delay, and the hazard of events; let me ask

---

*Declaration of Independence.

the man, who can raise his mind to one elevated conception, who can awaken in his bosom one patriotic emotion, what judgment ought to have been pronounced by the impartial world, by the friends of mankind, by every virtuous citizen, on the conduct and character of this assembly? Or if there be a man whose propensity to condemn is susceptible of no control, let me then ask what sentence he has in reserve for the twelve states who *usurped the power* of sending deputies to the convention, a body utterly unknown to their constitutions; for congress, who recommended the appointment of this body, equally unknown to the confederation; and for the state of New York, in particular, who first urged, and then complied with this unauthorized interposition?

But that the objectors may be disarmed of every pretext, it shall be granted for a moment, that the convention were neither authorized by their commission, nor justified by circumstances, in proposing a constitution for their country: does it follow that the constitution ought, for that reason alone, to be rejected? If, according to the noble precept, it be lawful to accept good advice even from an enemy, shall we set the ignoble example, of refusing such advice even when it is offered by our friends? The prudent inquiry in all cases, ought surely to be not so much *from whom* the advice comes, as whether the advice be *good*.

The sum of what has been here advanced and proved, is, that the charge against the convention of exceeding their powers, except in one instance little urged by the objectors, has no foundation to support it; that if they had exceeded their powers, they were not only warranted, but required, as the confidential servants of their country, by the circumstances in which they were placed, to exercise the liberty which they assumed; and that finally, if they had violated both their powers and their obligations, in proposing a constitution, this ought nevertheless to be embraced, if it be calculated to accomplish the views and happiness of the people of America. How far this character is due to the constitution, is the subject under investigation.

PUBLIUS

to be continue...

www.ingramcontent.com/pod-product-compliance
Lightning Source LLC
Chambersburg PA
CBHW031430210526
45464CB00005B/2142